Children of Poverty

Studies and Dissertations on
the Effects of Single Parenthood,
the Feminization of Poverty,
and Homelessness

Stuart Bruchey
UNIVERSITY OF MAINE
General Editor

A Garland Series

Prevention in Child Welfare

States' Response to Federal Mandate

Krishna Samantrai

Garland Publishing, Inc.
New York & London
1993

Library of Congress Cataloging-in-Publication Data

Samantrai, Krishna, 1938–
    Prevention in child welfare : states' response to federal mandate / Krishna Samantrai.
        p.   cm. — (Children of poverty)
    ISBN 0-8153-1126-5 (alk. paper)
    1. Child welfare—United States—States. 2. Federal aid to child welfare—United
States.   I. Title. II. Series.
HV741.S26   1993
362.7'0973—dc20   92–32111
                                                                   CIP

Printed on acid-free, 250-year-life paper
Manufactured in the United States of America

CONTENTS

LIST OF TABLES

INTRODUCTION

Public responsibility for the care of destitute, neglected, and abused children has been a social issue in American history since the time of the early settlers. From the seventeenth through the nineteenth centuries orphan, pauper, neglected or abused children were placed in out-of-home care with substitute families or in institutions. In the early twentieth century, care of poor children underwent a revolutionary change, from out-of-home care to care in their own homes. With Illinois taking the lead in 1911, several states passed Mothers' Aid laws, providing pensions to (suitable) widowed or deserted mothers so that children could stay at home instead of being placed with substitute families. This principle of economic assistance to mothers to prevent out-of-home placement of children was extended to all states in 1935 when, under Title IV of the Social Security Act, federal government provided grants to states for the Aid to Dependent Children program. Over the years Title IV has been amended several times, and though there are wide variations between states, providing economic support, however meager, to families of children who have no other means of economic support has become an established social program.

For neglected and abused children, however, removal from their own homes and placement in foster care[1], whether in homes or institutions, continued as the dominant and in some jurisdictions the only form of care. Between 1950 and 1980 several studies on foster children identified the problem now known as "foster care drift" (Maas and Engler 1959; Jeter 1963; Children's Defense Fund 1978; Fanshel and Shinn 1978; Shyne and Schroeder 1978; National Commission on Children in Need of Parents 1979). These studies confirmed that children were often being placed in foster care unnecessarily because there were no alternative services for even simple difficulties faced by the family. Foster care, intended to be temporary, was indeed not temporary at all. Once placed in foster care, children were likely to remain there until the age of majority, often being moved from one foster home to another, usually without regard to their needs. There was no monitoring of placements to assess either the appropriateness or the continuing need for placement. Contact with biological families was cut off, thus severing family ties. There was no aggregate data at any level of government about children in, or facing, foster placement. A root cause of this problem was identified to be the federal policy framework that provided unlimited funds to states for out-of-home placement of children without any accountability requirements (except judicial determination that staying at home was contrary to the welfare of the child), but no funds to provide alternative assistance to families.

The idea of providing supportive services to families to prevent unnecessary placement of children in out-of-home care, which began to develop in the 1950s, culminated in the enactment of The Adoption Assistance and Child Welfare Act of 1980 (also referred to as P.L. 96-272 or the Act). The primary objective of P.L. 96-272 is to ensure permanency for children, by preventing their entry into the foster care system, or, if they must be placed for reasons of their safety, by moving them out of foster care as quickly as possible, either facilitating their return to their own homes under safer conditions or facilitating their adoption. To achieve this objective, P.L. 96-272 mandates supportive services to families by the child welfare system and provides adoption subsidies for hard-to-adopt children.

P.L. 96-272 reflects a major change in the philosophy and goals of child welfare. Traditionally, child welfare involved child protection, foster care, and adoption services, that is, *out-of-home care services for children* whose families could not, for whatever reason, care for them according to the prevailing norms of society. P.L. 96-272 mandates *supportive services to families* so as to *prevent* unnecessary out-of-home placement of children. To stimulate states to implement this change, P.L. 96-272 adopts a carrot-and-stick approach, providing federal fiscal incentives to states for development of preventive services, and imposing fiscal sanctions if such services are not in place by the time the Act is fully funded for two consecutive years.

But a new federal administration came in very shortly after the enactment of P.L. 96-272 with a completely different political agenda — to minimize federal role in domestic policy and return authority to the states. It did not provide the intended fiscal incentives for implementation of supportive services to families. In addition, it reduced Title XX funds for all social services and eliminated the state match requirement. A national economic recession further reduced the states' own resources while increasing their need for human services.

This reduction in federal funds was found to have varying effects on development of prevention programs in the states in the first two years of the Act. Oregon maintained an exemplary program and reduced its foster care population to those children who were most difficult to help, those with most problems requiring higher cost care and longer time in care. New York allocated $24 million of its own funds to develop or expand the capability for delivering a variety of preventive services. California and Texas traded prevention for crisis services. Michigan and Kentucky were struggling to maintain some preventive services (Koshel and Kimmich 1983). The Koshel and Kimmich study identified variation in states' prevention effort during the two-year period following the enactment of this Act, but it did not explain the reasons for or identify factors, if any, associated with this variation.

So far, neither the federal funding nor the states' economic situation has improved much. Under these circumstances, to what extent is this change being implemented in the states? Is there a variation, in FY 1985-1986, in states' child welfare expenditures and prevention effort? Is this variation totally random, or are there any explanatory factors? Is this legislation perceived by states as incentive for development of prevention programs? These questions motivate and guide this study.

Theoretical Context

This study utilizes the conceptual model of implementation developed by Van Horn and Van Meter as its theoretical guide. The dependent variables were identified as the state's child welfare expenditures, its prevention effort, and its perception of incentive. Based on the theoretical model and review of related research, four independent variables were identified — characteristics of the state's implementing agency; the state's political and ideological environment; disposition of its implementors; and its economic and social conditions (needs and resources). Six propositions and hypotheses were developed. First, in FY 1985-86 states varied in their child welfare expenditures and in their prevention effort, when measured as dollars per child or as staff time on prevention activities. Second, variation in states' child welfare expenditures and in prevention effort was related to the characteristics of its implementing agency, its structure and status in the state government. Third, variation in states' child welfare expenditures and its prevention effort was related to its political and ideological environment. Fourth, variation in states' child welfare expenditures and in prevention effort was related to the disposition of its state-level implementors — that is, the extent to which the state governor, key state legislator, and the director(s) of the state agency responsible for child welfare services agreed with the social values embodied in P.L. 96-272.

Fifth, variation in states' child welfare expenditures and in prevention effort was related to its social and economic conditions. And sixth, states did not perceive P.L. 96-272 as incentive for development of primary prevention services for children and families.

Design

This is an exploratory study with single cross-sectional survey design in which the unit of investigation is the state. Data were collected through a questionnaire mailed to the administrator of the designated child welfare agency (or another person in the agency nominated by the administrator) in each of the fifty American states and the District of Columbia. States' demographic and budgetary data were obtained from secondary sources. Both parts of the study instrument are included in the Appendix. Data thus gathered were analyzed using univariate, bivariate and multivariate statistical procedures.

Implications of This Study for Social Work Practice

Professional social work has a historic commitment to the welfare and well-being of children and families; it has often taken an active and leadership role in influencing public social policies to improve the quality of life for children and families. This role, however, has generally been based on values, ideology, and case information. As such, influencing the formulation of such policies has been a monumental task in the context of American social and political values. Experience has shown that even when legislation is enacted, its intent is not necessarily achieved in its implementation.

In recent years in particular, the need to influence both the formulation and the implementation of social policy has been felt more acutely by the professional social work community. However, efforts based on ideology and anecdotal or case information have proven to be of limited effectiveness, and there is little empirical knowledge to guide such practice. The traditional evaluation research approach, useful in evaluating the effectiveness of specific programs, has been of little utility in this endeavor as it does not analyze the personal agendas and political environment in which social policies are implemented.

The implementation approach accepts the existence of multiple organizational and personal agendas in the political and social environment within which social policies must be implemented. It identifies an array of factors that are significant to the success or failure of a particular policy or program, thus providing an empirical basis for strategic intervention and manipulation of those elements over which control and influence can be exercised. In adopting the implementation approach to the study of a policy that has fundamental implications for public social services to children and families, this study hopes to provide an empirical basis for the practice of social work in the policy arena, and to stimulate further interest in development of theory to guide such practice.

Organization of the Report

The historical context in which P.L. 96-272 came to be enacted and its relevant sections are discussed in Chapter I. This chapter also reviews selected literature on the concepts of "prevention" and "perception of incentive." Study of implementation, development of various conceptual models and related research studies, and the rationale for the selection of Van Horn and Van Meter's conceptual model as a guide for this study are discussed in Chapter II. Methodology is discussed in Chapter III; descriptive and statistical findings are discussed in Chapters IV and V respectively. In the final chapter, conclusions and implications for the practice of social work in influencing the formulation and implementation of policies affecting services to children and families are discussed.

Prevention in Child Welfare

I
Review of Literature

Historical Context

Roots of the practice of out-of-home care of children can be traced back to Elizabethan Poor Laws of sixteenth-century England, which established the use of indenturing and apprenticeship as methods of caring for pauper children. Early settlers in the American colonies continued this practice in the New World. In the nineteenth century, the number of children needing out-of-home care began to increase. Indenturing no longer sufficed, so institutional care evolved. Providing assistance and services to biological families so they could keep their children did not occur to even the most devout reformers of the time. On the contrary, rescuing children from their (inadequate) families and providing substitute care for them was considered to be the best form of child welfare practice.

The value of biological home life for children was a discovery of the early twentieth century. Delegates to the first White House Conference on Children in 1909 went on record with the statement "Home life is the highest and finest product of civilization. . . . Children should not be deprived of it except for urgent and compelling reasons" (Bremner 1971:365). Informed welfare workers affirmed that poverty alone was not sufficient cause for removing children from their own homes. In the next two decades several states passed Mothers' Aid laws, providing pensions to suitable widowed or deserted mothers so their children could stay home with them instead of having to be placed out.

Cautious beginnings having been made in the early twentieth century, the principle of federal responsibility for services to children and families was established with the Social Security Act of 1935. Title IV established the Aid to Dependent Children program, whereby federal government shared 33% of the cost of subsidies to children in single-parent families, with eligibility and benefit levels left to the discretion of the states. Under Title V, Part I provided grants for Maternal and Child Health; Part II provided grants for Crippled Children's Services; and Part III, Child Welfare Services, provided grants to states to establish, extend and strengthen, especially in predominantly rural areas, public welfare services to protect and care for the homeless, dependent, and neglected children as well as children in danger of becoming delinquent.

The definition of child welfare services expanded over the years and restriction to rural areas was lifted in 1958. Federal funds for these services, however, determined by the Congressional budgetary process and distributed to the states as formula grants, were always a token amount, generally used by the states to supplement their resources for child protection and foster care services. Despite the rhetorical recognition in federal policy that children at risk of or in out-of-home placement could benefit from preventive child welfare services, federal money was never sufficient to be an incentive to the states to create such services.

The Aid to Dependent Children program began as and continues to be a federal entitlement program. It became Aid to Families with Dependent Children (AFDC) in 1950 when an allowance for the caretaking parent was added. In 1961 Louisiana eliminated 22,000 children from its AFDC eligibility because of their "unsuitable" home, without making any alternative provisions for them. Advocates of children were outraged by this action. In response to their efforts, federal government extended the AFDC program to foster families and child care institutions when the child was placed out-of-home upon judicial determination that the home was unsuitable. In a major reform effort in 1967, this extension was mandated in all states. In addition, federal participation level was increased (Title IVA), and child welfare services were combined with the AFDC program as a strategy to help families get off the welfare rolls (Title IVB). In the implementation of these reforms, an unintended consequence emerged. Since federal government shared the cost of foster care but not the cost of services to families that would prevent foster care, it was cheaper for the states to place and keep children in foster care. Fragmentation in community services hindered families' own efforts to obtain needed services before crisis developed, and when it did, foster care was often the only alternative available to them. Once a child was placed in foster care, there were no financial resources or incentives for programs to assist families with the problems that necessitated placement. Foster care allowances were also a disincentive to adoption.

The plight of children in foster care first came to light with the publication of Maas and Engler's (1959) exploratory study of foster children in nine selected communities between October 1957 and August 1958. This study found the problems now known as foster care drift—the unnecessary placement of children in out-of-home care, their lingering and drifting in foster homes until the age of majority, often forgotten by the system that placed them, the severing of family ties. The Children's Bureau study (Jeter 1961), and several studies thereafter confirmed the findings of the Maas and Engler study. These problems began receiving increasing attention from professionals, child welfare advocates and officials. At the same time, there were several successful programmatic attempts, primarily on demonstration basis, both to prevent placements and to ensure permanence for children in placement (Jones, Magura and Shyne 1981). The decade of the 1960s was also a period of increasing attention on the rights of disenfranchised groups, including children. Throughout the 1970s, efforts to modify state and local policies were hampered by the aforementioned disincentives for keeping children with their biological families. As the significance of federal framework in aggravating the problems of foster children became clear, it became obvious that major federal reforms would be necessary if children in foster care, or those at risk of out-of-home placement, were to have any permanence in their lives.

The opportunity for reform came with the issue of baby-selling, which began to receive media attention and aroused some public outrage. In April 1975, the Senate Subcommittee on Children and Youth held hearings on baby-selling, followed in July by hearings on adoption of special needs' children. In these hearings, testimony addressed the barriers in the broader child welfare system that left many families without children, and many children lingering in foster care, and the role that federal policies played in creating these barriers. In March 1977 Representative George Miller introduced the Comprehensive Child Welfare Reform Bill which eventually became P.L. 96-272.

P.L. 96-272: The Adoption Assistance and Child Welfare Act of 1980

P.L. 96-272 replaced, as of 1 October 1982, the Title IVA AFDC-Foster Care Program with a new Foster Care and Adoption Assistance Program under Title IVE of the Social Security Act, and amended the Title IVB Child Welfare Services Program. This Act embodies and represents national commitment to the principle of permanency planning for children.

The concept of permanency planning takes as its major premise that the child's well being must be paramount in any service plan. In order to ensure this, children must have a home in which they feel a sense of belonging and permanent membership, to guarantee the continuity of relationships essential for development of positive self image, the establishment of healthy relationships with others, and the ability to function well in society. This suggests that the biological family is primary to the care and upbringing of children, for it is here that an initial sense of belonging and membership is first developed. Disrupting this tie is a major decision — one that must not be made unless there is evidence that serious harm will come to the child if left at home. If the situation is serious enough to warrant the child's removal from home, it is incumbent upon the agency that removes the child to provide an alternative for the child in which these needs can be met, and to do restorative work with the family. If restorative work with the family is not successful and the biological family cannot resume care of the child, a home intended to last indefinitely must be found, either through termination of parental rights and placement of the child in an adoptive home, or through planned long-term foster care in a single home which allows the child to develop substitute parental ties (Goldstein, Freud and Solnit 1973). According to Pike (1977), permanency describes intent. A permanent home is not one that is guaranteed to last forever, but one that is intended to exist indefinitely. Permanency planning thus holds promise of maintenance of biological families for children, restoring children in care to their biological families in a timely fashion, or finding other permanent homes for children who cannot return to their biological families.

P.L. 96-272 defines child welfare services as:

> public social services directed toward the accomplishment of the following purposes: (A) Protecting and promoting the welfare of all children, including handicapped, homeless, dependent or neglected children; (B) preventing or remedying, or assisting in the solution of problems which may result in, the neglect, abuse, exploitation or delinquency of children; (C) preventing the unnecessary separation of children from their families by identifying family problems, assisting families in resolving their problems, and preventing breakup of the family where the prevention of child removal is desirable and possible; (D) restoring to their families children who have been removed, by the provision of services to the child and the families; (E) placing children in suitable adoptive homes, in cases where restoration to the biological family is not possible or appropriate; and (F) assuring adequate care of children away from their homes, in cases where the child cannot be returned home or cannot be placed for adoption (Sec. 425. a.).

It establishes, in policy, the scope of public responsibility to children.

Acceptance of public responsibility to assist and maintain biological families and *prevention* of out-of-home placement of children represents a major shift from the traditional practice of indefinite foster placements of children. To stimulate states to develop needed changes, P.L. 96-272 adopts a carrot-and-stick approach. Part E of this Act authorizes "such sums as may be necessary" for federal payments for foster care and adoption assistance. To qualify for such payments, however, states must demonstrate that removal of the child from the home was the result of judicial determination that continuation of living at home was contrary to the child's welfare, and that reasonable effort was made, a) prior to the placement of a child, to prevent or eliminate the need for removal of the child from his home; and b) if the child was removed, to make it possible for the child to return to a safer home as quickly as possible [2]. Part B of this Act provides funds for child welfare services as defined above, authorizing $163.35 million for FY 1981, $220 million for FY 1982, and $266 million for FY 1983 and FY 1984. (Authorization for 1979-1980 was $141 million.) These funds were to be distributed to the states according to the existing formula — each state to get a base of $70,000; the remainder of the appropriated money for the year to be divided between states with each state's allotment based on the ratio of its child population to that of the rest of the country. This method of distribution was to be used until the appropriations reached $141 million, the 1979 authorization level. But when the appropriations exceeded $141 million, the additional allotment to a state was contingent upon its having conducted a one time inventory of all children in care for six months or longer to determine the necessity and appropriateness of current placement; the implementation and satisfactory operation of a statewide information system containing the status, demographic characteristics, location, and goals for each child; the implementation and satisfactory operation of a case review system that monitored the progress of the child at least once every six months and offered due process protection to parents before termination of their rights; and the implementation and satisfactory operation of a service program to help children either return home or be adopted. If a state had not instituted these programs as well as a preplacement prevention service program designed to help children remain with their families by the time of full funding of the Act for two consecutive years, its share of the allotted money was to revert back to its 1979 level.

Prevention of out-of-home placement of children, thus, is a major objective of P.L. 96-272. To support this new thrust toward strengthening families and providing permanency for children, P.L. 96-272 included amendments to the Title XX social services program, progressively increasing authorizations each year, requiring a 25% state match, and earmarking $200 million, full federal funding, for day care services.

Prevention

Prevention is a familiar term in its use in the old adage — an ounce of prevention is worth a pound of cure. As a concept it is simple and sensible, a principle about which there is little disagreement. In practice in human services, it is inherently complex, with little agreement about its definition or its operationalization.

To prevent means to keep from happening. The American Heritage Dictionary defines it as "to anticipate and keep something (undesirable) from happening by means of prior action." With regard to social problems, this concept is not new. Indenturing and placing children with foster families was supposed to prevent economic dependency and delinquency. Nineteenth-century societies were formed and programs were developed to prevent such social problems as poverty, alcoholism, cruelty to and exploitation of children.

The popular conceptualization of prevention, however, derives from the field of public health. The public health model developed around the turn of the century, when control of acute infectious diseases was its primary preoccupation. Based on the assumptions that there is a single causative agent which can be isolated and studied in the laboratory, an identifiable point of onset and course of disease with predictable symptoms or manifestations, their impact on various parts of the body and ultimate outcomes, and that there is an identifiable "population at risk" — actual or potential victims of the disease — this model identifies three levels of activities. Primary prevention refers to elimination of the causative agent at its source through destruction of its habitat, or through immunization of the population at risk. Secondary prevention involves efforts to curtail the spread of disease to others and to interrupt its course through early identification and treatment. Tertiary prevention aims to reduce the duration and severity of the disabling sequelae. Thus, all public health activities are subsumed under this umbrella concept of prevention.

Developing as a profession in the early years of the twentieth century, social work adopted this model and developed its methodology and expertise in "treatment" of specific, identified problems (secondary prevention) and "rehabilitation" (tertiary prevention). Prevention was conceptualized along two continua: the time dimension, and degree of pathology. Any intervention taken earlier rather than later, to catch a disorder at the time of onset or during mild disturbance, was defined as prevention.

Interest in the concept of prevention revived in the 1950s with the debate about the function of professional social work in industrial society. Proponents of the residual function advocated the role of social work as amelioration and direct service to relieve stress and social breakdown. Proponents of the institutional function argued that in an industrialized society change is rapid and ever present, so that concern is not only with stress and social breakdown but with the viability of human response and adaptation. They argued that the forces of industrialization and urbanization have changed the nature of essential old institutions like the family, but the needs met by such institutions continue, and rapid change creates other new needs. Society, therefore, must in the normal course of industrialization guarantee and institutionalize the means to assure that essential old functions are discharged in new ways and that new functions are recognized as legitimate responses to new circumstances. Social welfare and social work services therefore need to be a regular, ongoing, and essential feature of the modern, industrialized society (Kahn 1979).

The National Association of Social Workers appointed a Subcommittee on Trends, Issues and Priorities to give clarity to the conceptualization of prevention and to find a definition that would give impetus to newer modes of practice. In its deliberations, this Subcommittee discarded the definition of prevention as "keeping something from happening," arguing that because most social work activities are launched after a problem has become manifest, such a definition would exclude practically all of social work and would cause the profession and the public to lose sight of the genuine preventative elements in much of social work practice. They considered distinguishing between self-maximization activities, preventative activities, and treatment activities, but discarded this approach because it excludes the preventive aspects of treatment of persons with serious pathology. They adopted a broader definition, namely "Prevention in social work is defined, then, as activities which have merit in averting or discouraging the development of specific social problems, or in delaying or controlling the growth of such problems after they have presented beginning symptoms" (Beck 1959:11). They proposed three levels of activities similar to the public health model. The first level, referred to as primary prevention, included health promotion and specific protection, undertaken before the "disease" attacks. The second level, referred to as secondary prevention, included early diagnosis and prompt treatment, undertaken in early stages of the "disease." The third level, tertiary prevention, undertaken in advanced stages of the "disease," included disability limitation and rehabilitation.

Rapaport (1961) disagreed with this position of the Subcommittee. In taking this position, she argued, social work has embraced the public health model in an undiscriminating and distorted manner. In affirming that since all social work activities are dedicated to the proposition that a condition must be kept from getting worse therefore all social work activities are in the nature of prevention, or at least have preventive components, the Subcommittee made treatment and prevention coterminous. She further argued that since all of society's growth promoting social institutions — family, school, health institutions, church and organized recreation — play a key role in the well-being of individuals, they all become relevant in preventive intervention. Taking a developmental or life-task perspective, she advocated activities such as income maintenance, family life education, day care, homemaker services, increased parental visiting in pediatric hospitals and earlier adoption. She perceived the social work practitioner as an advocate of the client and as consultant to programs in agencies, hospitals and other social institutions to which people are connected.

Dissent with the application of the public health model of prevention to the fields of social work and mental health has been expressed by practitioners and theoreticians since the early 1970s. They have argued that the sickness and disease model of public health is not applicable to social and mental health problems, since these problems arise from complex, multiple, interrelated social and psychological factors rather than from a single causative agent. Addressing the prevention of child abuse and neglect, Giovannoni (1982) argues that the classic public health model is not even applicable to diseases that are not acute and infectious, much less to a problem like child abuse and neglect in which none of the assumptions of that model apply. These practitioners and theoreticians posit that preventive intervention should not be defined to be less than, earlier or more than traditional curative interventions, but as a different activity that derives from new perspectives, that emphasizes wellness, health and growth (Klein and Goldston 1977; Bloom 1980, 1981; Adam 1981).

This conceptualization of prevention, however, raises problems in implementation. Primary prevention, as Bloom describes, "deals with problems that don't exist, with people who don't want to be bothered, with methods that probably haven't been demonstrated to be efficacious, in problems that are multidisciplinary, multifaceted and multigenerational, involving complex longitudinal research designs for which clear-cut results are expected immediately for political and economic reasons unrelated to the task in question" (1981:8). Gilbert (1982) discusses three policy issues in primary prevention: identification of the target group, unanticipated consequences, and the problem of implementation. When problems exist, those experiencing the problem are identified, either by themselves or by others in the community, and services can be directed towards them. But when problems don't exist, who is to make the judgment that any particular group is in need of primary prevention, and how are the issues of social stigma, negative self-image, and possibility of self-fulfilling prophecy to be addressed? Since there are always limits to the knowledge of social sciences, the possibility of unanticipated undesirable consequences also exists, as became evident in the poverty programs of the 1960s. And finally, in transferring the technology of prevention from experimental pilot projects with circumscribed populations to larger regions or the nation, planners have to make certain that professional standards of services provided by well-trained, highly motivated professional staff of the pilot project are maintained for continued effectiveness.

Along with the problems of values and implementation are the complications of the American political system. Legislation in this country springs from a perceived need usually fostered by advocacy groups centered on solving a specific problem or reflecting a specific categorical area or services. Primary prevention is a comprehensive concept which cuts across categorical areas; its definition implies the concepts of wholeness and interrelatedness which are far more complex and difficult to comprehend than discrete, categorically circumscribed areas of life. Such complexity deters development of specific political constituency to advocate policy, programs and funding. Because primary prevention cuts across categorical areas, coordination becomes essential — between agencies, within communities, and between professionals, volunteers and citizen leaders. This requires a willingness to plan, set priorities, share responsibilities, and identify causes that extend beyond individuals or single agencies. This can challenge personal and organizational freedoms. Requiring an investment and commitment to the future as opposed to short-term results, primary prevention is incompatible with the political need to show immediate, short-term results (Hastings 1982). All these issues become even more critical in the field of social services to children and families, which is fraught with conflict around the role of government in family life.

Because of this nature of primary prevention, governments find it easier to finance programs for existing problems rather than for programs that are likely to prevent problems from occurring. The child welfare community lobbied for P.L. 96-272 so that there would be federal pressure on states to develop and implement prevention programs. In American federalism, however, governmental authority is divided between federal and state governments. Welfare and well-being of its citizens are the right and responsibility of the state governments; in this arena the federal government has no right to make decisions or issue directives to the state governments. Since the federal government does not have the power to order the state governments, it seeks to influence them by offering incentives in the form of grants and attaching conditions to them, which they may or may not accept. In its domestic programs the federal government has used the grant-in-aid system to stimulate additional public services at state and local levels and to support national minimum standards (U.S. Advisory Commission on Intergovernmental Relations 1978).

For this system to be effective, federal incentives must be perceived as such for the states to accept them. Insufficient or inappropriate incentives have caused the failure of several social programs. One example is the attempt by the Johnson administration to create new model communities on federally owned lands in metropolitan areas (Derthick 1972). In the summer of 1967 the Johnson administration offered federal land to the local governments to build low and moderate income housing. The expectation was that the incentive of land, in addition to the existing federal aid of grants for planning, urban renewal and housing construction would produce results. Four years later, no new communities had been built; practically none had even been started. A number of state and local factors such as weak mayors, racial concerns, and clashes between conservationists and urban planners created roadblocks that could not be surmounted by the additional incentive of federal land. Another example is the federal Economic Development Administration's program to create 3000 jobs for the hard-core unemployed in Oakland, California. A sum of over $23 million was made available as grants and loans to public and private projects, the condition being that they include a plan for employment of the hard-core unemployed. Numerous participants were involved: the Port of Oakland, which was to develop its marine terminal and an industrial park; World Airways, who agreed to lease the terminal and the facilities at the industrial park; the U.S. Navy, who used the existing terminal and the access waterways to it; and the city government, which was to provide the land for the industrial park, build the access road to it, and provide public transportation for the target population who lived downtown to get to work at the industrial park. Decisions and actions of each participant were contingent upon the decisions and actions of other participants in the form of a causal chain, the end result of which was to be jobs for the unemployed. Federal money was not a sufficiently strong incentive to overcome the complex political, economic and bureaucratic forces generated by this program (Pressman and Wildavsky 1979).

Perception of Incentive

Barnard's theory of inducement and Etzioni's concept of compliance contribute to an understanding of what might be perceived as appropriate and sufficient incentives. According to Barnard (1968), organizations need individuals' contribution in order to survive. Individuals have two basic motives to contribute — self-preservation and self-satisfaction. To induce people to contribute, the organization must appeal to these two motives. Individuals will contribute if their net satisfactions are high enough for them. Barnard presents this as an equation: net satisfaction = positives or advantages - negatives or disadvantages. The organization can either increase the positives or decrease the negatives, but often a distinction between the two is not possible. A more important distinction, however, is between the subjective and objective aspects of inducements. By objective, he implies the tangible and intangible things such as wages, conditions of work, opportunity, and status. By subjective, he implies the state of mind, attitudes, and motives. The organization cannot always offer enough objective incentives to suit the existing state of mind of the individual; its alternative then is to change the state of mind through persuasion, rationalization, or coercion so that the available incentives will be enough. Even though material rewards have been inculcated as a value and an ideal in our society, these by themselves are usually not sufficient inducement beyond a certain point, once basic needs of living have been met.

Etzioni (1965) proposes that different kinds of organizations require different kinds of compliance systems. Where participants in an organization are alienated and have an intense negative orientation towards the organization, coercive power—the application or threat of punitive sanctions — may be required to achieve adherence to organizational objectives. Where most participants have intense positive orientations and are highly committed to the organization's goals and objectives, compliance can usually be achieved through the use of normative power — the allocation and manipulation of symbolic rewards and deprivations. Where participants do not have intense orientation towards the organization but their involvement is a function of perceived costs and benefits, remunerative power — the allocation of material resources — is likely to be the most effective means of achieving compliance.

In federal-state relations, then, sufficiency and appropriateness of incentive will depend upon the orientation and the relative power of key individuals and groups in the states. And it will depend upon the perceived costs and benefits, both tangible and intangible, to the state.

By offering grants and attaching conditions to them, the federal government changes the balance of costs and benefits to the state. It causes the state to consider whether the required action should be taken, if indeed the value of the grant offered is more than the cost of conditions and possible penalties attached to it. For state political actors (elected or appointed legislative or executive officials, party officials, pressure groups) who independently share some or all of the federal goals, such a federal action creates opportunities for the making of proposals. For possessors of authority within the state government, whether elected officials or appointed administrators, federal sponsorship reduces the cost of making a proposal and taking the subsequent action and at the same time increases the cost of inaction — the cost of not proposing or taking the actions the federal government seeks to stimulate. Not only are monetary costs transferred to the federal level; if opposition arises, political costs can be transferred as well by assigning responsibility to the federal government. Officials who do not respond to federal stimuli become vulnerable to criticism for failing to act, for failing to take advantage of federal funds, or failing to meet federal standards.

Federal influence, however, operates mainly through the state agency that receives and administers the federal grant. One of the basic conditions of a federal grant is that the state designate a single agency within the state government which would receive and administer the grant. In requiring that this agency possess sufficient authority to assure that federal conditions are met, federal administrators contribute to the state agency's power and autonomy within the state government. In the interest of its own existence and power within the state government, this agency must act in ways that will ensure the continuation and, if possible, the enhancement of federal funds it receives. The state agency thus becomes an instrument of the federal government and an ally to the extent that it shares, or is willing to adopt the values, programmatic goals, and interests of the federal government, along with undertaking the required actions. In formulating and implementing its regulations and administrative procedures to meet the federal requirements, the agency can also becomes an influencer of state policy.

An unintended consequence of the pursuit of any federal goal through the grant system is the production of state and local behavior that is directed towards increasing federal funds rather than towards federally prescribed programmatic ends. Derthick (1970) argues that this phenomenon of goal displacement in organizational behavior is a common one, by no means uniquely the product of the grant system; but by elevating the receipt of federal funds into the motivating principle of action, the grant system as a mode of governmental conduct encourages this phenomenon. She states that the limits on federal ability to directly influence the behavior of recipient agencies indicates the great importance of indirect influence, through indoctrination of state and local administrators so that their values and program objectives will be the same as those of federal administrators.

The extent to which any federal grant is perceived as incentive for change thus depends upon certain features of a state's political and administrative system — the prevalence of values consistent with federal actions; the presence of federal allies; the power of those allies in state politics; the prevailing ideology or political culture; and the state's receptivity to federal action generally. To achieve results, therefore, federal officials must have enough knowledge of local politics to perceive what incentives are necessary; they must supply the incentives in sufficient quantity; and they must direct the incentives to those holders of local power whose support is required to achieve the federal purpose (Derthick 1972).

Summary

The traditional approach to addressing the problem of children whose parents are unable to care for them according to the prevailing norms of society has been to remove the children from their families and place them in out-of-home care. Traditional child welfare practice thus involved child protection, foster care, and adoption. Developments in the 1950s — concern about children lingering and forgotten in the foster care system and programs demonstrating that alternative services to families in trouble could prevent unnecessary separation of children and families — combined with the 1960s' movement towards rights of disenfranchised groups, including children, and the baby-selling scandal of the 1970s culminated in the enactment of P.L. 96-272 in 1980. This Act represents a dramatic change in the goal and philosophy of child welfare, from focus on child protection and out-of-home placement of children to focus on families and *prevention* of unnecessary out-of-home placement of children.

Prevention, however, is a concept difficult to operationalize in the context of American social values and political system, and state governments generally find it easier to implement programs for existing problems rather than programs to prevent problems. P.L. 96-272 was enacted as a means of inducing states, through a system of federal fiscal incentives and sanctions, to develop prevention programs. But for federal incentives to be effective, they have to be perceived as such by the states. To be perceived as incentive for change, they have to be appropriate to the political, administrative and ideological climate of the state.

II
THEORETICAL CONTEXT

Implementation, Theory and Conceptual Models

A major lesson of the 1960s, the decade of federal legislation for social welfare, was that enacting a policy and allocating federal funds do not automatically lead to resolution of social problems. Failure of social programs to achieve the desired objectives drew the attention of social scientists to the process of implementation, which Hargrove (1975) called the "missing link" in policy and program analysis.

In the Webster and Roget dictionary, "implement" is defined as "to carry out, accomplish, fulfill, produce, complete." In one of the first studies on implementation of social policy, Pressman and Wildavsky (1979) raised the question: is implementation just a fancier name for administration? In this and several subsequent studies, implementation has emerged as an integral part of both policy formulation and administration, a critical link between them. It has been defined variously as the "stage between a decision and operation, the next hard step after the decision, involving efforts to operationalize what has been decided" (Williams 1980:1); "the terrain between inputs and outputs, the question of how policies change as they are translated from administrative guidelines to practice" (Rein and Rabinovitz 1977:1); "decisions made in carrying out a policy" (Montjoy and O'Toole 1979:465); and "those actions by public and private individuals or groups that are directed at the achievement of objectives set forth in prior policy decisions" (Van Horn and Van Meter 1976:45).

The earliest perceptions of implementation were shaped by the classical model of public administration that gained widespread publicity in the 1930s. Based on the concepts of ideal bureaucracy (Weber), separation of politics and administration (Woodrow Wilson), and scientific management and efficiency (Taylor), this model assumes that policy-making and policy implementation are bounded, separate, and sequential. Policy makers

17

make decisions regarding goals, and implementors carry them out in a technical, non political manner (Nakamura and Smallwood 1980). These authors state that at least three developments led to the reexamination of this view of implementation. First, a number of studies in decision making during the 1950s indicated that policy formation was more complex than this model assumed, that making decisions was, in many cases, too complex and subtle to involve the clear-cut type of policy choices and specificities implied in this model. Second, additional studies in public administration and organizational behavior indicated that the implementation of policy was also much more complex than was previously thought, and that the process of administration is influenced by an intricate variety of psychological norms and bureaucratic pressures that take on a complex political life of their own. The third development was the disillusionment with the Great Society programs in the mid-1960s, when it became apparent that it might be easier to legitimize social policy by passing ambiguous legislation than to carry it out by means of effective program implementation.

The flurry of academic interest started with Pressman and Wildavsky's case study of the Federal Economic Develoment Administration's project to create jobs for the inner-city unemployed in Oakland in 1966. Since then, implementation has been studied at the point of policy-making, with exhortations to policymakers to consider implementation when making policy decisions; at the point of administration from the perspective of the implementing organization; and at the point of service delivery from the perspective of the service delivery worker. Conceptual models identifying different factors that impede successful implementation have been developed. Each of these models describes one facet of implementation; each facet, though significant and relevant, provides only a partial explanation of the implementation process. A more comprehensive theoretical model was developed by Van Horn and Van Meter in 1976. These authors theorize that effective implementation depends, in part, on the nature of the policy, but specific factors contributing to the realization or nonrealization of objectives vary from one policy type to another. This model was selected as the theoretical guide for this study as it incorporates the multiple factors and their interaction in the implementation of policies requiring intergovernmental participation. In this chapter, the partial conceptual models of implementation and related research are discussed as a prelude to the more detailed discussion of Van Horn and Van Meter's model and the theoretical framework guiding this study.

Partial Theories

The Causal Chain Model

According to Pressman and Wildavsky (1979), policies are hypotheses containing initial conditions and predicted consequences. They imply theory. Whether stated explicitly or not, policies point to a chain of causation between initial conditions and future consequences. Policies become programs when, by authoritative action, initial conditions are created. Programs operationalize theory by forging the first link in the causal chain connecting action to objectives. Implementation, then, is the ability to forge subsequent links in the causal chain so as to achieve the desired results.

Using the causal chain analogy and probability theory, they argue that the longer the chain, the larger the number of decision points, the lower the probability of achieving the objective. Their major recommendation thus is simplicity and directness, to reduce the length of the chain and the number of decision points. They conclude that implementation should not be divorced from policy and should not be conceived of as occurring after, and independent of, the design of policy; and that careful consideration should be given to the theory underlying action. Finally, they recommend that as much attention be paid to the creation of organizational machinery to execute a program as to launch one.

Implementation as Political Process

Bardach (1977) views implementation as a political process. His conceptualization is based on the study of implementation of the Lanterman-Petris-Short Act in California in the early 1970s. This Act was intended to protect the civil liberties of persons alleged to be mentally ill and to accelerate the trend for community treatment of the mentally ill as an alternative to institutionalization in remote state hospitals.

Bardach views policy or program in motion as a blueprint for a large machine. The elements that go into this machine depend upon the specification of what this machine was supposed to do and where it was to be located. These elements, however, are held and controlled by many different parties, most of whom are in important ways independent of each other. The only ways to induce them to contribute their elements is through persuasion and bargaining — essentially the political process. Implementation, according to Bardach, is the process of assembling the elements required to produce a particular programmatic outcome, and the playing out of a number of loosely interrelated games whereby these elements are withheld from or delivered to the program assembly process on particular terms. These games deflect goals, divert resources, dissipate energies and resist initiative. Therefore, he recommends strategies to avoid the games altogether, such as designing simple programs that require as little management as possible and manipulating prices and markets rather than writing and enforcing regulations. He also recommends a "fixer, " a politician with power to produce results and provide demonstration of interest through continued oversight.

Rein and Rabinovitz (1977) developed a model encapsulating existing experience. They also view implementation as a political process, from the point of view of strategizing the behavior of various actors, but the process is characterized by the principle of circularity. They conceptualize implementation as "1) declaration of governmental preferences, 2) mediated by a number of actors who 3) create a circular process characterized by reciprocal power relations and negotiations" (1977:8). Their model posits three stages of policy implementation: guideline development, resource distribution, and oversight; and three imperatives that operate at each of the three stages: the legal imperative, to do what is legally required; the rational-bureaucratic imperative, to do what from a bureaucratic point of view is administratively feasible, morally correct and intellectually defensible; and the consensual imperative, to do what is necessary to attract agreement among contending influential parties who have a stake in the outcome. The politics of implementation, they argue, may be best understood as an attempt to resolve conflict between these imperatives. The need to reconcile these potentially conflicting imperatives at each of the three stages sets up the process of circularity that characterizes the implementation process.

Implementation as Management Problem

Williams (1980), on the other hand, recommends better agency mangement. In the study of the Comprehensive Employment and Training Act of 1973 and the Community Development Block Grant programs of the Nixon administration, Williams introduces the concept of "shared governance," joint jurisdiction and programmatic responsibility between two or more layers of government. He argues that shared governance has created an uneasy partnership in which the negative powers of each partner to block and harass the other are much stronger than the positive powers to move in the desired direction. Grants-in-aid that provide funds to another political jurisdiction but charge the federal agency with management responsibilities make that uneasy partnership more amenable to influence than to control, for when local entities deliver services, federal government and indeed all governments face severe limits to their power to control the direction of social service delivery programs. A host of socioeconomic, technical, political and bureaucratic forces interact to create bewildering problems that reduce an organization's capacity to govern the program it must administer and operate. Williams thus proposes a two-pronged framework of analysis: the limits of power — political or bureaucratic factors; and resources — monetary and technical knowledge, authority, staff expertise, time and organizational structure. For better implementation, Williams urges political executives to devise management strategy that redistributes agency resources in order to increase local commitment to federal performance objectives and local capacity to deliver services.

Implementation as Organizational Problem

Since governmental programs are implemented by organizations, Montjoy and O'Toole (1979) posit that it is useful to conceptualize implementation as an organizational problem. According to these authors, some of the problems in implementation can be predicted from the nature of the policy and the intra-organizational problems that could result from new patterns of activity required when an external mandate is assigned to an established agency. They developed a model that can be used to analyze prospective policies in terms of their implementability. In this model, three characteristics of the organization and two characteristics of the policy are used. The organizational characteristics are, first, the dominant coalition, with a consistent set of preferences (goals) and beliefs about cause-effect relationships (world view); second, the constraints on the ability of the dominant coalition to direct agency activities imposed by a set of external mandates and existing routines; and third, the resources to bring about changes in routines by new mandates — funds, staff, time, and expertise. The two characteristics of the policy are its specificity and the amount of new resources accompanying it. For the sake of simplicity they dichotomized these variables to yield four possible types of policy mandates:

| | | Characteristic of Mandate | |
		Vague	Specific
	Yes	A	B
New Resources			
	No	C	D

Montjoy and O'Toole argue that Type A Mandate, vague with new resources, creates the highest degree of discretion which will be used according to the goals and worldview of the dominant coalition. If no dominant coalition exists, opportunity will be passed on to others. Type B mandate, specific with new resource, is most likely to provide opportunity for necessary changes in organizational routines to carry out the mandate. Type C mandate, vague with no new resources, is likely to produce little new activity. Compliance with vague mandates can be interpreted as occurring within existing routines, which act as constraints in the absence of new resources. Type D mandate, specific with no new resources, imposes the constraints of both the existing routines and the specific policy mandate, leaving little discretion to leadership. However, if the agency resources are being fully used and there is little slack, new demands will compete with existing ones and leaders will have to establish priorities. Such a mandate therefore, in effect, increases discretion. Montjoy and O'Toole hypothesize that the way this discretion is used will depend on the strength and direction of forces within the organization. When there is unanimity in the organization, it may respond with defiance, appearance of activity (for example, decked reports), and/or make a token effort and then record the difficulties in implementation. When the organization is not unanimous and there is no strong dominant coalition, the new mandate becomes a resource and a catalyst for the formation of a new dominant coalition. Or, the leadership might use the mandate for some totally unrelated purpose.

Related Research

Some of the earliest studies of the formulation of public policies were undertaken by political scientists. They investigated the relationship between political systems and public policies and found that higher interparty competition was related to more progressive public policies. Dawson and Robinson (1963) added the variable of economic factors to this bivariate relationship in a study of nine public welfare policies in the American states. They defined welfare policies as programs that directly or indirectly redistribute wealth. Using four revenue policies (percent revenue from death/gift taxes, percent revenue from federal government, per capita amount of state revenue, and tax revenue in relation to personal income) and five expenditure policies (per pupil expenditures, Aid to Blind, Aid to Dependent Children, Unemployment Insurance, and Old Age Assistance) in their study, they found that interparty competition did not play as influential a role in determining the nature and scope of welfare policies as earlier studies suggested; the level of public social welfare programs in the

American states seemed to be more a function of socioeconomic factors, especially per capita income. High levels of interparty competition were highly related to both socioeconomic factors and to social welfare legislation, but the degree of interparty competition did not seem to possess the important intervening influence between socioeconomic factors and liberal welfare programs.

Collins (1967) analyzed a cross section of 1964 state data for four public assistance programs (Old Age Assistance, Aid to Families with Dependent Children [AFDC], Aid to Blind, and Aid to Permanently and Totally Disabled) to see if variations among states in expenditures, recipient rates, and average payments could be explained by objective economic factors. She concluded that only a fraction of the variation could be explained by objective economic and demographic factors. The remainder reflected differences in attitudes among state and local governments, economic factors peculiar to each state which could not be measured fully, and random elements. She found that public assistance expenditures rose with the income level of the state; average payments were higher in wealthier states while recipient rates were higher in poorer states; and that in every public assistance program, controlling for income and urbanization, average payment declined as the fraction of nonwhite population increased. States that were more generous in one assistance program were also generous in others, and federal participation in financing the programs proved to exert an equalizing fiscal influence among states. Urbanization had only a mild influence on public assistance payments.

In her study exploring states' commitment to AFDC, Ozawa (1978) found great differences in the level of AFDC payments in states. Statistically significant determinants of maximum monthly payments in the state, identified through a stepwise regression analysis, were found to be percent nonwhite population, the strongest predictor, having a negative relationship, and the per capita personal income and the state's tax effort, both having positive relationship with the dependent variable. These three variables explained 64% of the variance. Other independent variables (unemployment rate, combined state percentage of children below 17 and aged population above 65, AFDC child recipient rate, extent of urbanization, and density of population) together explained only 1.2% of the variance.

Levels of mental health expenditures were also found to vary greatly in the states between 1977 and 1983 (Hudson 1987). Measuring need as the state's suicide rate and crime index, this study investigated the role of the state's (1) geographic location and population characteristics; (2) taxation system, wealth, and federal assistance, and (3) governmental structure, citizen participation, and administrative capacity in its mental health spending behavior between 1977 and 1983. Collins' and Ozawa's finding of the strong role of per capita income in welfare expenditures was confirmed, but percent nonwhite population was not found to be significant. States' mental health spending behavior was also found to be related to its geographic region, the extent of citizen participation, progressive taxation, type of organization, and the power of the governor over appointment of the state mental health director.

Bullock and Lamb (1984) examined seven civil rights policies across ten implementation variables. They found that in policies in which there was greater federal activity, such as voting rights and school desegregation, implementation was more successful once the federal government shifted from passive to active enforcement. Success in implementation decreased as the extent of federal involvement decreased, as illustrated by the employment, bilingual education, higher education, housing, and second generation discrimination policies. The most important variables were found to be federal involvement, specific standards, agency commitment, support from superiors, and costs and benefits. Clarity of policy goals was found to be only somewhat important. They argue that while ambiguity may prevent maximum implementation, changes in employment and bilingual education suggest that some progress can be made even when policy goals are imprecise, and that this pattern supports the hypothesis that federal involvement determines the extent of implementation when the objectives are as unpopular as those of civil rights.

A review of these studies supports Van Horn and Van Meter's theory that specific factors affecting the realization or nonrealization of objectives vary from one policy type to another. In the implementation of income maintenance policies such as Old Age Assistance, Aid to Blind, or Aid to Disabled about which there is little or no value conflict, the state's economic conditions appear to be the most significant variable. As agreement about the goals of the policy decreases and ambivalence and value conflicts increase — for example, AFDC and Civil Rights policies — variables like percent nonwhite population, state political and organizational factors, and the extent of federal involvement become more significant. Mental health policy appears to fall somewhere in between; even if there is little goal consensus, services may have to be provided if the need is high — if not for ideological reasons then for reasons of social protection.

Toward a Comprehensive Theory:
Van Horn and Van Meter's Model

Van Horn and Van Meter (1976) developed a more comprehensive framework for analyzing policies that require the participation of various governmental units. This conceptual model is used as the theoretical guide to this study.

The basic premise of this model is that the probability of effective implementation will depend, in part, on the nature of the policy, but specific factors contributing to the realization or nonrealization of objectives will vary from one policy type to another. To analyze the nature of the policy, Van Horn and Van Meter use two characteristics, goal consensus and the amount of change required. They dichotomize these variables to yield four possible types of policies:

		Goal Consensus	
		High	Low
	Major	1	2
Amount of Change			
	Minor	3	4

They suggest that implementation will be more effective when minor changes are required and goal consensus is high. Furthermore, policies involving major change / high consensus are more likely to be implemented more effectively than those involving minor change / low consensus, and goal consensus has greater impact than the amount of change required for policy implementation. With these hypotheses in mind, they developed a model of intergovernmental policy implementation that identifies eight variable clusters and relationships among them. These are:

1. Policy.
    a. Resources: adequacy and timing.
    b. Standards and objectives: quality, clarity, consistency and accuracy.
2. Linkages.
    a. Communication.
    b. Enforcement.
    c. Political conditions: extent of support or opposition in public and elite opinion.

    d.   Characteristics of the implementing agency: experience and competence of staff, status within parent organization or local government structure.

    e.   Disposition of implementors: their orientation and belief in goal/objective of the policy.

    f.   Social and economic conditions: needs and resources.

(see diagram below)

Van Horn and Van Meter's Theoretical Model of Intergovernmental Policy Implementation

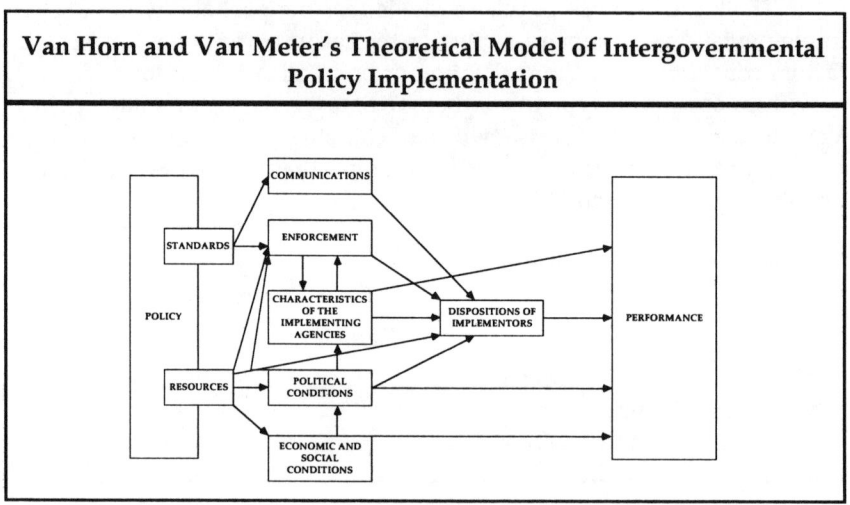

The Policy: Resources and Standards

Policies provide financial and other resources for programs and their administration and enforcement. Implementation often fails when funds and incentives are not adequate. In addition, the timing of the release of funding information to the agency can have important consequences for the success of the program; administrators who are forced to plan with insufficient knowledge about the amount of funds will often experience serious difficulties. Agencies that are faced with severe budgetary cutbacks will perceive and carry out their tasks quite differently from those that enjoy expanding budgets. Policy resources may influence the environment where implementation occurs by supporting and empowering interested individuals and groups to press for full implementation and successful policy performance.

Policy standards move beyond the general legislative goals and establish requirements, in varying degrees of specificity, for how policy goals shall be implemented. Policy standards tell federal, state, and local implementors what is expected of them and indicate the amount of discretion left open to them. They also provide overseers with tools of influence and enforcement, since they set limits on the types of activities that are tolerable, and on the sanctions that can be imposed for deviations. Standards may remain vague because policymakers are unable or unwilling to reach a consensus on the directives to be promulgated, or ambiguities may be fostered deliberately in order to ensure positive responses by implementors.

Communication

Policy standards cannot be complied with unless they are communicated with sufficient clarity so that implementors will know what is required of them. While good communication will not necessarily contribute to a positive disposition on the part of implementors, variations in their support for the policy may often be explained in terms of their understanding and interpretations of the policy standards and the manner by which they are communicated.

Enforcement

Successful implementation usually requires mechanisms and procedures that increase the likelihood of implementors acting in a manner consistent with policy standards. Federal officials have essentially three means of achieving compliance from state and local officials: norms, incentives, and sanctions. These correspond to Etzioni's (1965) distinction betwen normative, remunerative, and coercive forms of power, discussed in the previous chapter. Federal officials, thus, must be sensitive to the characteristics of the state they are dealing with when they consider means of ensuring compliance with their objectives.

Political Conditions

The extent of support for or opposition to the policy objectives by organizational superiors and by public and private individuals and groups influences implementation efforts and results, regardless of the positions of the implementors or the quality of the agency executing the program. Where the problems to be remedied by a program are severe and private citizens and interest groups are mobilized in support of a program, it is more likely that implementors will accept the policy's goals and objectives. On the other hand, the impact of federal enforcement activities may be mitigated when state and local implementors are opposed to certain aspects of the policy and can enlist the support of organizational superiors or their congressional delegations.

Characteristics of the Implementing Agencies

The formal and informal attributes of the organization responsible for implementation affect its ability to carry out the policy standards. No matter what the attitudes of its personnel, their experience and competence to perform the tasks required of them, and the status of the agency — either within the parent organization of which it is a part or the local government structure — will tend to limit or enhance the prospects for effective implementation.

Disposition of Implementors

The success or failure of many federal programs has often been attributed to the level of support enjoyed within the agency responsible for implementation. Implementors may not execute the policy's standards because they disagree with or reject the objectives contained in them for a variety of reasons: the objectives may offend the implementors' personal value systems, self-interest, organizational loyalties or existing preferred relationships. The intensity of implementors' response may also affect the implementation process; those holding intense negative orientations towards the policy may openly defy program objectives while persons with less intense attitudes may attempt surreptitious diversion and evasion.

Social and Economic Conditions

Economic conditions, both as needs and resources, influence the chances of successful program performance. Depending upon the types of need within a community, the implementors may be led to accept or reject certain goals of the policy or its approaches. Likewise, the extent of need may influence otherwise negatively oriented officials to embrace the policy in order to minimize public hostility or to respond to public wishes.

Types of resources of the community will also influence the kinds of services that can be offered and their importance. Some areas may have the capacity to carry out public services without federal assistance. If federal requirements are objectionable, they may refuse to participate in the program altogether.

The Implementation of P.L. 96-272

The use of this theoretical model in the study of the implementation of P.L. 96-272 leads first to an examination of the nature of the policy itself. It then leads to the hypotheses that the implementation of the prevention mandate depends upon the two policy variables — resources and standards; and the six linkage variables — communication, enforcement, states' political conditions, characteristics of implementing agencies, disposition of implementors, and states' social and economic conditions.

The Nature of P.L. 96-272

Child welfare policy is not as accepted and conflict-free as Old Age Assistance, Aid to Blind, and Aid to the Disabled. It shares some of the characteristics of mental health policy in that if need is high, services have to be provided for reasons of social protection in addition to humanitarian and ideological reasons. It also shares some of the characteristics of civil rights policy in that it involves basic values and conflicting philosophies regarding the care and protection of children that are rooted in our history. There is no widespread consensus on the role of government in family life or the responsibilities of various levels of government. The amount of change required is high; where federal policy used to support out-of-home placement of children, which has been our historical tradition, it now requires the *prevention* of out-of-home placement of children by providing supportive services to families. Like AFDC policy, our commitment to this goal is ambivalent at best. The prevention mandate of P.L. 96-272 thus is a Type 2 policy involving major change and low goal consensus; the likelihood of it being implemented effectively, therefore, is low.

Policy and Linkage Variables: Resources, Standards, Communication and Enforcement

P.L. 96-272 authorized progressively increasing appropriations for child welfare services, from $141 million in 1979 to $266 million in 1984. In addition, authorization of Title XX social services funds were increased progressively from $2.7 billion in FY 1980 to $3.3 billion in FY 1985 and thereafter. States were required to provide a 25% match; $200 million were earmarked for day care services (Russell 1984). The intent thus was to increase the states' capacity to provide services and at the same time provide sufficient incentive for them to do so.

In developing regulations for implementing the new provisions, the Department of Health and Human Services (HHS) solicited public input through public meetings, regional hearings, and written comments from child advocates. HHS and the advocates believed that regulations must be sensitive to state practices yet specific enough to ensure consistency in interpretation and uniformity in implementation. The proposed regulations exemplified the best professional practice in child welfare. And they spelled out what constituted adequate compliance with programmatic requirements so that states had a standard to measure themselves against. State compliance with these requirements was to be determined by reports submitted to HHS and by on-site surveys conducted before the awarding of any incentive monies (Federal Register December 31, 1980).

In January 1981, however, the new Reagan administration suspended all recently issued regulations under the Carter administration, thus canceling the proposed rules under P.L. 96-272. In February, the White House released its agenda for economic recovery, proposing massive cuts in human services, creation of block grants, and equally massive increases in defense spending. These fundamental policy changes were put in place with the Omnibus Budget Reconciliation Act of 1981 (OBRA).

In 1981 and again in 1982, the Reagan administration tried to repeal P.L. 96-272 and merge it in the general social services block grant; each time this proposal was rejected by Congress. During this time, federal funds earmarked for day care were eliminated, and funds for Title XX programs were reduced to $2.4 billion, an amount $100 million lower than when the program was first created in 1975. Requirements for state match and federal standards for child care and day care were also eliminated. Regulations for the implementation of OBRA appeared in the Federal Register on October 1, when this law became effective, but regulations for P.L. 96-272, passed a year earlier, were not issued until May 23,1983. In the formulation of the new regulations, HHS declined to require public participation and ignored most of the comments it received from child advocates regarding specific and detailed regulations. The new regulations did not specify even a minimum level of services that had to be provided as requirements for states to receive incentive funds (Federal Register May 23 1983; Russell 1984).

In this process the Reagan administration communicated its intention of not taking any role in inducing change in states' child welfare services. It was not going to provide necessary resources and did not really care whether or not the states provided any resources. It was not going to set any minimum standards, therefore, there was little to enforce.

Study Variables

For the states, then, there was little variation in these four policy and linkage variables. Against this common backdrop, the variables likely to influence variation in implementation in states were their political conditions, characteristics of their implementing agencies, disposition of their implementors, and states' social and economic conditions.

These four variables lead to four hypotheses. First, variation in states' child welfare expenditures and prevention effort would be related to their political and ideological environment. Second, variation in states' child welfare expenditures and prevention effort would be related to characteristics of their implementing agency — its structure and status in the state government. Third, variation in states' child welfare expenditures and prevention effort would be related to the disposition of major implementors; and fourth, variation in states' child welfare expenditures and prevention effort would be related to their social and economic conditions. These hypotheses are based on the proposition that states vary in their child welfare expenditures and in their prevention effort. In addition, the nature of the policy and the nature of the four federal-level variables discussed above (resources, standards, communication, and enforcement) lead to the proposition that the states did not perceive P.L. 96-272 as an incentive for the development of primary prevention services.

These four antecedent variables and six propositions and hypotheses form the theoretical framework for this study.

Summary

The model of implementation developed by Van Horn and Van Meter forms the theoretical guide to this study. These authors theorize that successful implementation will depend, in part, on the nature of the policy, but specific factors contributing to the realization or nonrealization of objectives will vary from one policy type to another. Their model consists of eight variable clusters and the relationships among them. In the implementation of P.L. 96-272, four variables — resources, standards, communication, and enforcement — were the same for all states; as such, the other four variables and the hypotheses derived from them and from the nature of the policy form the theoretical context of this study. Other conceptual models that explain the implementation process partially and related research are also discussed in this chapter as a prelude to the discussion of Van Horn and Van Meter's theoretical model.

III
METHODOLOGY

Research Design

The purpose of this study was to investigate the extent to which the prevention mandate of P.L. 96-272 was being implemented in the states, in view of the fact that the expected federal fiscal incentives were not forthcoming, federal funds for all social services were reduced, and the states' own fiscal situation was very constrained because of the general economic recession during this period. This study intended to explore and describe the variation in states' child welfare services and prevention effort since the enactment of P.L. 96-272, and associated state factors that could explain this variation. Focus was on implementation at the state level in terms of the state policy and administrative context which determined the opportunities and constraints of local agencies, the ultimate deliverers of service, not on implementation in terms of actual services delivered at the local level.

Two alternative designs were given careful thought. One was a case study of four to six states known for their relative presence or absence of strong preventive programs. This study would have built on the Koshel and Kimmich study of 1983 by analyzing the states they used, two having allocated their own resources to strengthen and develop preventive services (Oregon and New York); two on the other extreme providing mainly crisis services only (California and Texas); and two in between, struggling to maintain some preventive services (Kentucky and Michigan). This design was rejected because its findings could not have been generalized to the other states, and because of financial and time constraints of the researcher. Alternatively, a survey design was considered and ultimately chosen. All fifty states could be surveyed so the findings of the study could be extended to most of the states, and a combination of mailed questionnaire and telephone interviews could be used to obtain data from each state. This design was feasible given the time and economic constraints that confronted the researcher.

The decision, based on these considerations, was to survey all fifty states. Indian Territories were excluded because their child welfare services are under the jurisdiction of a different federal legislation. Other Territories were excluded because they were too different in their social, economic and political characteristics to make them comparable to the American states. A longitudinal study by this researcher was neither feasible nor necessary. Therefore, a simple cross sectional design was selected. The year 1985 was selected as the study year because this was the most recent year for which data was available for this study in 1986-87.

Sample

The state policy and administrative context could be investigated from the perspective of key individuals at the state level or at the local level or both. At the local level, the local administrators, direct service providers, and the recipients of services could have been sampled. Possibility of sampling the recipient population in all fifty states was discarded as being beyond the scope of this study. With the population of local administrators and direct service providers, sampling would have involved either a simple or stratified random sampling of the counties of all fifty states and then a simple or stratified random sampling of local administrators and providers in each county. But, both the size of the states varying from three counties in Delaware to two hundred counties in Texas, and the size of the staff varying from less than one direct service provider in rural counties to over a thousand in large urban counties would have imposed difficulties in drawing comparable random samples from all fifty states.

A focus on state-level actors appeared to be more feasible. The state officers who bear the ultimate responsibility for implementation of child welfare services in the entire state are the administrators of the designated state agency. They are accountable to the state government for efficiently meeting the child welfare needs of the state and to the federal government for fulfilling funding conditions and requirements. Thus they are crucially placed for interaction with local agencies, state political actors, and federal monitors. They also have the greatest objective knowledge of the state policy, planning priorities, resources and statewide programs and services. These administrators, therefore, were the logical people to be included in the study sample.

Another key individual at the state level is the legislator who oversees the implementation of the companion state law in the state legislature. Legislators are most familiar with the policy-making process, but their knowledge of policy's impact on the state administrative context and at local service delivery level varies depending upon personal interests and political realities of the state. The role of the key state legislator is an interesting antecedent variable to study, and according to one theoretical model, crucial to successful implementation (Bardach 1972). But the idea of including them in the study was rejected because it would have been difficult to secure access to legislators from each state. It was also decided not to contact the child welfare advocates and interested academics. Locating such persons in each state who were truly knowledgeable about the implementation process would have been difficult; in addition, controlling for variables like their motivation, and their power and influence in the state government would have been necessary.

Based on these considerations, it was decided to obtain data only from the administrators of the designated state agency. As they are public employees, the researcher expected a relatively high rate of participation. Since only one individual was to participate from each state, it was decided to include all fifty states and the District of Columbia in the survey.

A list of administrators of departments directly responsible for the administration of child welfare services within the state agency in each of the fifty states and the District of Columbia was obtained from the 1985-1986 Directory of American Public Welfare Association. These names, mailing addresses and telephone numbers were updated and confirmed by telephone calls to each administrator's office. In this first telephone call, an initial contact was made with the administrators. An introductory letter from the researcher's faculty chairperson was then mailed to each administrator in the updated list (see Appendix A). In this letter, the research and the researcher were introduced and the administrators' participation was requested. If they could not participate, they were asked to nominate another person in their department. Confidentiality was assured and an offer to share findings of the study was extended. They were not expected to respond to this letter if they did not wish to nominate another person. Thirty five responses were received to this request, of which five were confirmations of administrators' own names. The final list thus assembled consisted of fifty-one persons, one from each state. Joint names of two people sent from two states were treated as one unit each.

Data Collection

Data were collected from the administrators and from secondary sources. Part 1 of the study questionnaire was mailed to the administrators (or their nominees) as soon as their name was received in response to the introductory letter. Part 2 of the questionnaire was used by the researcher to gather demographic and budgetary data for each state and the District of Columbia from secondary sources (U.S. Department of Commerce, Bureau of Census 1980, 1986; National Conference of State Legislatures 1986; Highlights 1982, 1983, 1984, 1985).

About three weeks after the mailing of introductory letter, questionnaires were mailed to the administrators who did not respond to the introductory letter. An attached cover letter referred to the earlier introductory letter, explained the purpose of the research briefly again, and requested return of completed questionnaires in three weeks from date of mailing (see Appendix B). A self-addressed stamped return envelope was attached to each questionnaire. One week after the specified date, a telephone call was made to nonrespondents. Another copy of the questionnaire was mailed, with another personal letter, self-addressed stamped envelope, and another specified date, to those who had either not received it, or could not locate it (see Appendix C). To others, the seriousness of the researcher's interest was conveyed. This approach was used as officials in several states indicated that they received numerous mailed questionnaires from a wide variety of researchers. At this time, four states indicated that they would not be participating.

Three weeks later, another phone call was made to nonrespondents in which the seriousness of the researcher's interest was conveyed again, and an offer to mail another copy of the questionnaire, if necessary, was made. Three weeks after this phone call, a final letter was mailed to nonrespondents and to those who could not be reached directly by phone, for whom messages had been left earlier. In this letter they were asked only to advise this researcher regarding their wish or their ability to participate (see Appendix D).

A total of thirty-four responses were received at the end of this process (response rate = 66.66%). A personal note of thanks was mailed to each respondent as soon as the completed questionnaire was received (see Appendix E). Further clarifications and elaborations on the responses, when necessary, were obtained by telephone calls.

Instrument

The variables of interest in this study were three dependent variables: the state's child welfare expenditures, its prevention effort, and its' perception of incentive; and four independent variables: characteristics of the child welfare system in the state, the state's political and ideological environment, disposition of its' implementors, and its' socioeconomic conditions. Since no existing pretested instruments or scales to measure these variables were found in literature, a new questionnaire was constructed. The first part of this questionnaire was mailed to the study sample; the second part was used to collect data from secondary sources (see Appendix F).

The first part of the questionnaire began with its introduction as part of the study of influence of P.L. 96-272 on child welfare services in the states. It then defined child welfare services as *primary prevention services* — services that would be available to the general population, such as telephone hotline, family or parent drop-in center, community education and awareness programs; *preplacement prevention services* — services that would be provided to children and families identified to be at risk, for example through a report of child abuse or neglect, but the child was not removed from home; *reunification services* — services to children and families when the child was removed from home, but the plan was to return the child to the family as quickly as possible; and *permanency planning services* — services geared toward finding alternate permanent families for children when the biological family is unable to resume their care.

Questions were divided into three sections. Section one focused on the dependent variables. Respondents were asked questions regarding the changes in child welfare services in their state since the enactment of P.L. 96-272, and their opinion on the influence of the carrot (increase or potential of increase of funds) or the stick (potential of loss or restriction of funds) aspects of P.L. 96-272 in bringing about these changes. They were then asked for their state's child welfare expenditure for FY 1985-86 and the amount contributed to it by federal, state and local governments; an estimate of the proportion of time spent by direct service staff in their state on each of the component services (primary prevention, preplacement prevention, reunification and permanency planning services); and the priority given to these services in planning for the following year. A statement introducing these three questions acknowledged the difficulty of accurate answers to these questions and requested the best estimate of the respondent.

Section two focused on the child welfare system in the state, its legislative and organizational context. The first four questions in this section were geared towards the state law governing child welfare services, the year it was enacted and the extent to which it made provisions for preventive services and competence of the direct service staff to deliver these services. The next set of questions in this section were designed to measure five aspects of the state child welfare system — the status of the state agency in the state government; its size and complexity; power of the director to influence both the nature of child welfare services in the state and the budget allocations for these services; the extent of autonomy of local agencies in deciding the nature of child welfare services and the circumstances under which they would be delivered; and the extent of monitoring of the local agencies done by the state agency. The last question in this section asked about the changes in the child welfare system and in the influence of child advocates in the state since the enactment of P.L. 96-272.

Section three focused on the political and ideological environment of the state and the values of the four major implementors at the state level — the governor, the key legislator, director of the state child welfare agency and the director of the umbrella organization if the state child welfare agency was a part of a larger umbrella organization. Respondents were asked about their state's history and tradition of child welfare services; its receptivity to federal direction; media coverage of child welfare related issues in the previous three years and the extent to which it might have influenced services; and the extent of support in the state legislature for child welfare services generally and primary prevention services particularly from the governor, members of the state legislature, state and local government officials and public organizations. The last question in this section asked the respondent to rate, on a four-point scale, the extent to which they thought the four implementors named above agreed with the values of permanency planning embodied in the Act — the importance of the biological family for the child, the responsibility of government to preserve the biological family and for provision of alternate permanent family for the child if the biological family could not care adequately for the child even after help.

Part 2 of the questionnaire was used to collect data on each state from secondary sources. This data included total state revenue from federal government and from state taxes; total population of the state and population under eighteen by race; the number of reports of child abuse and neglect received per year since 1982; the number of children in out-of-home care; number of children in single-parent families; and the number of children living below the state's poverty level.

Validity and Reliability

Testing validity and reliability posed a major dilemma. Because of the nature and size of the study sample, a pilot study did not seem feasible. Therefore, face validity and content validity were sought formally through judgment of committee members and informally from some local administrators, active advocates and academic researchers in child welfare. Factual data obtained from federal government publications, national incidence studies, or directly from respondents were assumed to be accurate.

Data pertaining to respondents' opinion and estimates is subject to random error. However, effort was made to reduce systematic error by writing unambiguous questions, including more than one question to measure the variables, and providing clear instructions.

Data Analysis

Data thus gathered were analyzed using univariate, bivariate and multivariate statistics. All variables were measured at interval or ratio level so Pearson's correlation coefficient was used as measure of association. Regression analysis was conducted with variables found to be associated with two dependent variables, "expenditure per child" and "prevention effort." A .05 level of significance was used; however, because of the sample size being so small, attention is drawn to variables associated between .05 and .1 level of significance.

Measurement of Variables

Dependent Variables

Three dependent variables were measured in this study: child welfare expenditures, prevention effort, and perception of incentive. The variable child welfare expenditure was measured as four subvariables. The first was expenditure per child under eighteen. The second subvariable, child welfare expenditure as proportion of the total state expenditure gave an indication of the priority given to child welfare services in each state. The third subvariable was expenditure per child under fourteen; this was to test the assumption that child welfare services are generally directed towards younger children, since states tend to have other sources of funds for services for adolescents. The last subvariable was the proportion of federal, state and local government contribution to the state's child welfare expenditure. This was to explore states' reliance on federal funds for child welfare services and to test association between the state's source of funds and its prevention effort.

Prevention effort was conceptualized as expenditure per child on prevention services (primary and preplacement) and as proportion of time spent by direct service staff on these activities. Data on expenditures on primary and preplacement prevention services proved to be most difficult to obtain from majority of the responding states as states' budget and accounting systems do not track expenditures according to these categories.

Only fourteen of the thirty-four responding states provided data that could be used to estimate expenditure per child, but this data did not lend itself to any determination of dominant sources of funds for prevention activities. Because of the small number of states for which this measure was available it was not used as the indicator of prevention effort to determine any associations with the independent variables. Prevention effort, therefore, was measured as percent time spent by direct service staff on primary prevention activities and preplacement prevention activities. Though states do not necessarily account for staff time in terms of these categories, all states provided an estimate.

Perception of incentive was measured as the degree to which, in the respondents' opinion, the actual or potential increase of federal funds, or the actual or potential loss of federal funds under P.L. 96-272 was significant in influencing the change in child welfare services in their states. Respondents rated each of these as very significant, somewhat significant, or having little or no significance in increasing primary prevention, preplacement prevention, reunification and permanency planning services in their state.

Independent Variables

Based on the theoretical model, four independent variables were explored in this study. These included the characteristics of the implementing agency; states' political and ideological environment; disposition of its implementors; and its social and economic conditions.

Characteristics of the Implementing Agency

The implementing agency was conceptualized as the child welfare system of the state. Five organizational characteristics of the state's designated child welfare agency were analyzed as subvariables. The first was the status of the state agency in the state government. A state agency that was a separate agency or was a cabinet level department was considered as having a very high status and was given a value of 1. Where the state agency was part of a larger umbrella organization, those at the first level of the bureaucratic hierarchy were given a value of 2, those at the second level were given a value of 3, those at the third level were given a value of 4, and those at the fourth level or below were given a value of 5.

The second subvariable was size — the number of programs the umbrella organization was responsible for. Size was rated on a four-point scale, 1 indicating small organization (responsible for two to four programs) to 4 indicating a large organization, responsible for more than ten programs.

The third subvariable was the power of directors of the child welfare agency and the umbrella organization. Power was measured as the extent, as reported by the respondents, to which each director could influence the state's budget allocations to child welfare services and the nature of child welfare services in the state. Each of these items was rated on a four-point scale, from great extent (1) to not at all (4). The subvariable power was then computed as an interval level variable by aggregating the scores on these two items.

The fourth subvariable, autonomy of the local agencies, was analyzed to explore the degree of centralization in the state. Respondents were asked if decisions regarding what constituted "risk" to children and families, meriting intervention, and the degree of emphasis on prevention services, was made primarily at the local level or at the state level. Respondents rated local autonomy on each of these two items on a three-point scale, from high (1) to low (3). The subvariable autonomy was computed as an interval level variable by aggregating the scores on these two items.

The last subvariable was the extent of state monitoring of local agencies. The subvariable monitoring was based on two items; the mechanisms used by the state agency to supervise local agencies' compliance with state requirements, and the mechanisms used by state agency when local agencies did not meet state requirements. Each of the five supervisory mechanisms listed in the questionnaire (verbal reports, written reports, field visits by state officials, quality control/assurance, and other) was weighted according to the frequency of its requirement. Items required once a month were weighted 12; items required once a quarter were weighted 4; items required biannually were weighted 2; and items required once a year were weighted 1. Scores on this question could thus range from 0, no requirements, to 95, all five items being required once a month, once a quarter, biannually and annually.

	Per month 12	Per quarter 4	Biannually 2	Annually 1	Total possible (weight)
Written reports					19
Verbal reports					19
Field visits					19
Quality control					19
Other					19
Possible total	60	20	10	5	95

Each of the six compliance-seeking items listed in the questionnaire (written reprimand, verbal reprimand, threat of reduction of funds, sanctions, technical assistance and financial assistance) were weighted ten, for a total score of sixty, to give each of them the same total weight as the total weight of most frequently used supervisory mechanism. Scores on this question could thus range from 0 to 60.

The subvariable monitoring was computed as ratio level variable by aggregating the scores on these two items. Possible scores ranged from 0 to 155.

Political and Ideological Environment of the State

Five indicators of the state's political and ideological environment were analyzed. The first, state's history of child welfare services was measured on a four-point scale. Respondent's perception of the state as being a leader in child welfare services was rated 1; as having a history of extensive services but not necessarily a leader was rated 2; as being average was rated 3; and having a history of minimal services was rated 4. The next three indicators — state's receptivity to federal direction, media attention to child welfare issues in the state, and its influence on services — were also measured on a four-point scale, 1 indicating very high to 4 indicating low or none. The fifth indicator, public and elite support in the state for traditional child welfare services such as child protection, foster care and adoption, as well as for primary prevention services was further subdivided into five categories: governor's support, legislative support, support from state government officials, local government officials and from citizen groups. Each of these categories was measured on a five-point scale, 1 indicating very high support to 4 indicating little or no support, while 5 indicated opposition.

An index of political and ideological environment was created by counting the number of times a response of 1 or 2 was made on each of the five indicators. Possible scores on this index ranged from 0 to 28.

Disposition of Implementors

The state-level implementors were identified as the state governor, the key legislator, director of the designated child welfare agency, and director of the umbrella organization in states where the child welfare agency was part of a larger umbrella organization. Their disposition was analyzed as the extent to which they agreed, in the opinion of the respondent, with the four basic premises of P.L. 96-272 — the importance of the biological family for the child; the responsibility of the government to provide services to families at risk to prevent unnecessary break-up of families and to provide primary prevention services to all families; and the responsibility of the government to find alternate permanent homes for children whose families could not care for them even after help. These were presented as four statements in the questionnaire. Respondents were asked to rate each implementor on each statement on a four-point scale, 1 indicating strong agreement to 4 indicating strong disagreement. Possible aggregate score for each implementor thus ranged from 4 to 16.

Social and Economic Conditions of the State

The social and economic conditions of the state most relevant to this study were identified to be its need for child welfare services, its economic capacity, and the proportion of its nonwhite child population. Each of these three was measured as a separate ratio level subvariable. Proportion of nonwhite child population was computed from the 1980 census data. Economic capacity of the state was measured as its per capita revenue from federal government funds and from state taxes. Five indicators of the subvariable need were analyzed. The first was the proportion of child population in the state, child being defined as a person below eighteen years of age. Since the driving force behind P.L. 96-272 was concern for children in out-of-home care, proportion of state's child population in out-of-home care was used as the second indicator. A very large majority of children are placed in out-of-home care because of neglect or abuse at home, so the proportion of children involved in reports of neglect or abuse in 1985 was used as the third indicator of need. However, the risk of abuse or neglect has been found to be very high in single-parent families and in poor families. Therefore, proportion of children living in single-parent families, and proportion of children living below the state poverty level as defined in the 1980 census were also used as indicators of need. Finally, since theory indicates that no one cause explains child abuse and neglect and that it is caused by multiple factors in various combinations, an index of need was created using proportion of children involved in reports of neglect or abuse; proportion of children living below poverty level, and proportion of children in single-parent homes. These three indicators were used only because they are quantitatively measurable and this data was available from secondary sources. These indicators are not to be construed as any more significant than other social, personal or interpersonal factors that have been found to be associated with neglect or abuse of children. It was also fully understood that these three factors would be overlapping, that is, it was possible that some of the children would be counted in more than one of these categories. This index, therefore, is a crude rather than an exact measure.

Limitations

In addition to all the limitations inherent in a survey design, the major limitations of this study are that two of its three dependent variables ("prevention effort" and "perception of incentive") and two of its four independent variables ("political and ideological environment" and "disposition of implementors") are based on the opinions and estimates of a top official in the state. This official is presumed to be the most knowledgeable person in the state in this field and to have opinions or estimates that are based on sound information. The instrument for data collection was devised by the researcher; while great effort was made to reduce measurement error, the extent of this error is not known. Measurement of the subvariable "need" is not as accurate as one would have wished. Census data for each of the fifty states was available for the year 1980 only; subsequent census bureau studies are based on national samples that indicate national trends rather than an accurate change in each state. In using this data, an assumption was made that the change was distributed evenly among the states, and that this data could be used as a basis of comparison between states.

Findings of this study, therefore, need to be viewed as exploratory in nature.

Summary

This is an exploratory study whose purpose was to explore and describe the variation in states' child welfare expenditures and their prevention effort in the wake of enactment of P.L. 96-272, and the associated state factors that could explain this variation. Focus was on state-level policy and organizational context that provides the opportunities and constraints for service delivery. A single cross-section survey design with base year FY 1985-86 was used. Data were collected through a questionnaire mailed to the administrators (or their nominees) of the designated child welfare agencies in all fifty American states and the District of Columbia, and from secondary sources. Univariate, bivariate and multivariate statistical procedures were used to analyze the data received from the thirty-four states that returned the completed questionnaire.

In addition to the limitations inherent in a survey design, this study is limited by the small sample size and the somewhat crude rather than absolutely precise measurement of some of the variables.

IV
FINDINGS — DESCRIPTION OF THE DATA

This chapter summarizes and describes the data from the thirty-four states that returned the survey questionnaire. Part A describes the two dependent variables — child welfare expenditures and prevention effort. Part B describes the four independent variables — the nature of the child welfare system in these states; their political and ideological environment, the extent to which it was favorable for prevention services; disposition of state level implementors, their agreement or disagreement with the basic values of permanency planning; and states' need for child welfare services and the resources available to them to provide these services. Part C describes the changes in the nature and scope of child welfare services in these states since the enactment of P.L. 96-272 and the third dependent variable, respondent's perception of the significance of this Act in bringing about these changes.

A. Dependent Variables

Child Welfare Expenditures

This section describes the variation between states in the amount of money they expended on child welfare services, and the place of child welfare services in the total state budget. It then describes the extent of fiscal participation of different levels of government — federal, state, and local — in states' child welfare services.

As child welfare services are likely to be directed towards younger children and states are likely to have other sources of funds for services for adolescents, expenditure per child under eighteen as well as expenditure per child under fourteen were computed. The range and distribution of expenditures for the two age groups were similar and they were highly correlated ($r = .99$, $p < .0001$). Expenditure per child under eighteen, therefore, is used as the dependent variable.

The 1985-86 child welfare expenditures in the states in this sample ranged from $3.6 million to $560 million. When related to states' child population, expenditures ranged from $2.71 to $197.65 per child and averaged $64.03 per child. Half the states spent less than $61. 03 per child. The distribution (standard deviation 44.58) shows a wide variation between states. Fourteen of the thirty-four responding states (41.2%) spent less than $50 per child; of these one spent as little as $2.71 and seven spent between $10.00 and $24.99. Another fourteen states (41.2%) spent $50-100 per child, and four (11.8%) states spent $100-120 per child on child welfare services. The two states with the highest expenditures spent $153.60 per child and $197. 65 per child respectively (see Table 1).

Table 1
States' Expenditure Per Child on Child Welfare Services

| | States | |
$ per child	frequency	percent
2.71	1	2.9
10-24.99	7	20.6
25-49.99	6	17.6
50-74.99	7	20.6
75-99.99	7	20.6
100-124.99	4	11.8
153.60	1	2.9
197.65	1	2.9
Totals	34	100

Expenditure on child welfare services was a minuscule part of the total state expenditures. Eight states (23.5%) spent less than one percent, nineteen states (55.9%) spent about one percent and seven states (20.6%) spent about two percent of their total state budget on child welfare services. Thus, almost 80% of the states in this sample spent one percent or less of their total state budget on child welfare services.

Funds for child welfare services derived primarily from federal and state governments. Federal funds in the thirty-one states that answered this question ranged from 5% to almost 100% of child welfare expenditures and averaged 47.4% (standard deviation 23.7). In ten states federal funds constituted less than 35% of their child welfare expenditures; of these, three states received less than 10% from the federal government. In twelve states federal funds constituted between 42%-58% of state child welfare expenditures. In nine states over 60% and in two states over 80% of the money expended on child welfare came from the federal government.

State government funding was proportionately lower than federal funding. Ranging from less than 1% in two states to 89% in two states, state government funding averaged 44.6% (standard deviation 22.4). Of the thirty states that provided this data, twelve states contributed less than 40% to their total state expenditure on child welfare services. Of these twelve, two contributed less than 1% and two contributed between 12 and 15%. Another eleven states contributed 42%-58% of the funds to their child welfare services, and the remaining seven states contributed over 60% of funds to their child welfare services. Of these last seven, two contributed as much as 89% (see Table 2).

Table 2
Federal and State Government Contributions to States' Child Welfare Expenditure

	Federal		State	
	f	(%)	f	(%)
% contribution				
<1	0		2	(6.7)
5-9	3	(9.7)	0	
12-15	0		2	(6.7)
19-26	5	(16.1)	3	(10.0)
34-39	2	(6.5)	5	(16.6)
42-58	12	(38.7)	11	(36.7)
61-68	3	(9.7)	4	(13.3)
69-79	4	(12.9)	1	(3.3)
84-89	1	(3.2)	2	(6.7)
100	1	(3.2)	0	
Totals	31	(100)	30	(100)

There was little fiscal participation at the local government level. Of the thirty states that answered this question, nineteen (63.3%) did not require any local contributions. Six states reported between 2 and 6% , four states reported between 11 and 13% and only one state reported as much as 40% of its child welfare expenditures as having derived from the local governments.

In summary, great variation is observed between states in their expenditure per child on child welfare services and in federal fiscal support of states' child welfare services. Expenditure per child ranged from $2.71 to $197.65 with a mean of $64.03 and standard deviation of 44.59. Federal fiscal support ranged from 5% contribution to almost full funding of the states' child welfare services. In two thirds of the states in this sample, federal funds constituted from about half to almost all of the states' child welfare expenditures. State government funding was somewhat lower than federal funding and ranged from less than one percent to 89% of their total expenditure on child welfare services. Child welfare services represented a very minor part of the total state expenditures. In a large majority of the states in this sample local governments either did not contribute or contributed a very small proportion of funds to their child welfare services.

Prevention Effort

This section describes the variation in states' efforts to prevent out-of-home placement of children. It then compares states' emphasis on prevention with treatment, referred to as reunification services; and with rehabilitation, referred to as permanency planning services.

In this study, prevention effort is defined as both primary prevention services that are available to all families, for example telephone hotline, drop-in center, community education and awareness programs; and preplacement prevention services that are provided to children and families who are identified to be at risk, for example through a report of suspected abuse or neglect, but the child has not been removed from the family. One of the measures of prevention effort was state's expenditure per child on prevention services. Since usable data on this measure was only available for fourteen states, it was not used in statistical analysis, but it provides interesting information about differences between states. The other measure of prevention effort was the proportion of time spent by direct service staff on prevention activities.

States varied widely in their expenditure on prevention services. Ranging from $1.36 per child in one state to $119.76 per child in another state, expenditure on prevention averaged $34.87 per child (standard deviation 30.34). Seven states spent between $11.00 and $23.00 per child.

The other five spent, respectively, about $23, $36, $40, $64, and $74 per child. Half the states spent less than $23.27 per child.

An analysis of the expenditure on the two kinds of prevention services, primary and preplacement respectively indicates greater emphasis on preplacement prevention services than on primary prevention services. Expenditure on primary prevention services ranged from $0.14 to $59.88 per child and averaged $14.03 (standard deviation 17.47). Expenditure on preplacement prevention services also ranged from $0.68 to $59.88 per child but it averaged $21.54 with a standard deviation of 15.43. Half the states in this subsample spent $7.34 per child on primary prevention services and $19.09 per child, almost three times, on preplacement prevention services. Three states spent equal amounts, $0.68, $5.78, and as much as $59.88 on each kind of service respectively.

Thus, wide variation in prevention effort is observed in this small subsample of fourteen states. When expenditure on the two kinds of prevention services is considered separately, preplacement prevention services are observed to receive inordinately more resources than primary prevention services.

Reunification services which try to reunite children and families when the child is in out-of-home placement, and permanency planning services which are geared towards finding alternate permanent homes for children who cannot return to their biological families, are not defined as prevention in this study, but in social work literature they are often referred to as secondary prevention or treatment and tertiary prevention or rehabilitation. To compare states' emphasis on prevention with that on treatment and rehabilitation, their expenditure per child on reunification and permanency planning services were also computed. Relatively high expenditure existed for reunification services. States ranged from less than $1.00 per child in three states to about $107.00 per child in one state and averaged $22.93 per child (standard deviation 28.54). Half the states spent less than $16.00 per child. For permanency planning services, expenditure was less than for preplacement services and reunification services, but more than for primary prevention services. Ranging from less than $1.00 per child in one state to about $60.00 per child in another, it averaged $16.09 per child (standard deviation 17.609). Half the states spent less than $9.87 per child (see Table 3).

Table 3
States' Expenditure Per Child on Prevention, Treatment and Rehabilitation

	Prevention		Treatment/	Rehabilitation/
	Primary	Preplacement	Reunification	Permanency Planning
Range	0.14-59.88	0.68-59.88	0.00-106.48	0.68-59.88
Median	7.34	19.09	16.40	9.87
Mode	0.145	0.678	0.000	0.678
Mean	14.03	21.54	22.93	16.09
Standard deviation	17.47	15.43	28.54	17.61

These fourteen states thus expended higher amount of money per child on prevention services than on treatment or rehabilitation, but prevention services were targeted towards families who are already at risk rather than on primary prevention services. The trend in these fourteen states appears to be towards greatest expenditure per child on preplacement and reunification services, that is, on services to families whose children are either identified to be at high risk for out-of-home placement through a report of suspected neglect or abuse, or are already in out-of-home placement. Expenditure was least on primary prevention services, that is, services that would reduce the risk from developing in the first place.

The other measure of states' prevention effort was percent of time spent by direct service staff on primary and preplacement prevention services. This data, available on all thirty-four states, confirmed the data on the expenditure per child on prevention services.

States' prevention effort, which ranged from 15% of staff time in three states to 75% in two states, averaged 39.7% (standard deviation 18.21). In ten of the thirty-four states (29.4%), staff spent about one-fourth of their time on prevention services. In five states each (14.7%) staff spent about two-thirds, one-half and one-third of their time respectively on prevention services (see Table 4).

Table 4 **Prevention Effort: Percent Staff Time on Prevention Activities**		
	States	
% staff time	frequency	percent
15-20	5	14.7
25-28	8	23.5
30-36	5	14.7
40-50	8	23.5
60-70	6	17.6
74-75	2	5.9
Totals	34	100

Time on preplacement prevention services far exceeded the time on primary prevention services. On primary prevention services, staff time ranged between 0% in six states to 15% in another and averaged about 4%, with almost two-thirds of the states spending 5% or less. In contrast, time on preplacement prevention services ranged from 10% in one state to 70% in another, and averaged 35.5%. The majority of the states spent between one-fourth to one-half the staff time on preplacement prevention services.

On comparing prevention services with reunification services and permanency planning services, it was found that time on reunification services was somewhat less than, but comparable to the staff time expended on preplacement prevention services. Ranging from 15% to 56% it averaged about 33% of staff time. Time on permanency planning services, on the other hand, was less than on preplacement prevention and reunification services but much more than on primary prevention services. Ranging from 5% to 54%, it averaged about 27% of staff time (see Table 5).

Table 5
Percent Staff Time on Primary Prevention, Preplacement Prevention, Reunification and Permanency Planning Services

% staff time	Prevention				Treatment/ Reunification		Rehabilitation/ Permanency Planning	
	Primary		Preplacement					
0	6	(17.6)	0		0		0	
0.5-4.9	10	(29.4)	0		0		1	(2.9)
5-9.9	11	(32.4)	0		0		4	(11.8)
10-19.9	7	(20.6)	6	(17.6)	2	(5.9)	6	(17.6)
20-29.9	0		9	(26.5)	10	(29.4)	7	(20.6)
30-39.9	0		6	(17.6)	11	(32.4)	8	(23.5)
40-49.9	0		5	(14.7)	8	(23.5)	5	(14.7)
50-59.9	0		2	(5.9)	3	(8.8)	3	(8.8)
60-69.9	0		5	(14.7)	0		0	
70-79.9	0		1	(2.9)	0		0	
Totals	34	(100)	34	(100)	34	(100)	34	(100)

In summary, states' prevention effort varied widely, from 15% to 75% of staff time on prevention services. States spent a comparable amount of staff time on prevention and reunification or treatment services. But, whether measured as dollars per child or percent staff time, prevention effort was directed to a much greater extent towards families already at risk of out-of-home placement of children rather than towards the prevention of risk.

B. Independent Variables

This part describes data on the four independent variables — characteristics of the states' implementing agency; states' political and ideological environment in relation to child welfare services; the perceived agreement or disagreement of state-level implementors with the permanency planning philosophy; and the characteristics of the states' child population, states' need for child welfare services and their economic resources.

States' Implementing Agencies

The implementing agency is the designated state child welfare agency that implements the legislation through administrative rules, regulations and procedures. This section describes the pertinent features of the states' legislative framework and then describes five organizational characteristics of the state agency.

Legislation

In the American federal system, services to children and families are the responsibility of the state government. In this arena the federal government does not have a right to tell the states what they must or must not do, but it can offer money and attach conditions to it, which a state has the freedom to accept or reject. P.L. 96-272 offers money to the states for such services under certain conditions. Each state must enact its own legislation, companion to the federal Act, to meet the conditions and requirements for federal funding under P.L. 96-272.

Thirty-one states answered the set of questions relating to their state's legislation. Prevention services were mandated in less than half the states in this study. Fourteen states (45.2%) mandated preplacement prevention services; resources for them, however, were provided in nine states only. Primary prevention services, on the other hand, were mandated in four states (12.9%) only, but eight state laws provided resources for them. Reunification services were mandated in eighteen (58.1%) states and permanency planning services were mandated in sixteen (51.6%) states. Resources for each of these were also provided by nine states only.

An issue often raised is the professional competence and ability of direct service staff to fulfill their job responsibilities, in view of the immense complexity of human problems generally manifested in clients of public child welfare agencies. Twenty-two (64.7%) state legislations did not mandate any minimum qualifications for their direct service staff while the other twelve states mandated a college degree. Only three of these twelve required a college degree with social work or behavioral science major and only one required state licensure as social worker. Only two states mandated recruitment of bilingual staff.

In summary, the states' legislative framework generally did not provide clear guidelines for implementation of the mandate of prevention. Relatively few states mandated preventive services and the mandates were usually not accompanied by additional resources. Some states provided resources without mandating preventive services. Requirement of professional competence of direct service staff was rare.

Characteristics of the State Agency

These features of the states' legislation are translated into administrative rules, regulations and procedures by the state agency for implementation at the point of service delivery at the local level. This section describes three characteristics of the state agency that have impact on formulation of rules and regulations — its status in the state government, its size and complexity, and powers of the directors involved. It then describes two characteristics of state-local relations that have impact on the implementation of these rules and regulations — the degree of autonomy given to the local agencies and the extent to which they are monitored by the state agency.

Status

In most states, the child welfare agency was relatively highly placed in the state government structure. In three states the child welfare agency was either a cabinet level department or a separate department. In twenty-eight states the designated child welfare agency was part of a larger umbrella organization, fourteen of which were the states' public welfare departments. Within the larger umbrella organization, nineteen state agencies were on the first level of hierarchy, three were on the second level, four on the third level, and two were located on the fourth level of the bureaucratic hierarchy.

Size of the Umbrella Organization

The umbrella organizations encompassing the child welfare agency tended to be large. In eleven (32.4%) states it was responsible for the administration of more than ten programs, in seven (20.6%) states it was responsible for more than eight programs, and in eight (23.5%) states it was responsible for the administration of five to seven programs. The umbrella organizations were relatively small in only two states (7.1%) where they were responsible for two to four programs.

Power of Directors — Extent and Source

Power was defined as the extent to which, in respondents' belief, the director of the child welfare agency and the director of the umbrella organization could influence the state budget allocations for child welfare services, and the nature of child welfare services in the state. Respondents were asked to rate each director's influence on budgetary allocations on a four-point scale, 1 denoting very high power to 4 denoting no power, and each director's influence on the nature of services on a four-point scale, 1 denoting very high power to 4 denoting no power. An aggregate score of 2 thus denoted very high power while an aggregate score of 8 denoted no power.

The umbrella agency director was given an aggregate score of 2 by 57% of the respondents and an aggregate score of 3 by 18% of the respondents. Thus, in 75% of the responding states the director of the umbrella organization was perceived as having high degree of power over both the budget allocations and the nature of child welfare services in the state. The remaining 25% respondents gave a score of 4 to this director signifying medium degree of power. None of the states perceived this person as having a little or no power. This director was appointed by the state governor in thirty-two states. In two states this person was appointed by an elected Board overseeing the umbrella organization.

The director of the child welfare agency where this agency was not a part of an umbrella organization was also a governor appointee. In twenty-six of the twenty-eight states where this agency was part of an umbrella organization, this person was appointed by the umbrella agency director. In two states this was a civil service position. This person was given an aggregate score of 2 by 27.2% respondents and an aggregate score of 3 by 24.2% respondents. Thus, this director was seen as having high power in 51.4% states. In two states this person was given aggregate scores of 5 and 6, denoting only a little power. On further analysis, it was found that this director was perceived as having very high or high influence on the nature of services in all states, but in only nine states (27.3%) this person was perceived as having very high or high influence on the budget. In six states (18.2%) this director was perceived as having little or no influence on the state budget allocations.

Thus both directors were perceived as having considerable power in the state government, but director of the umbrella organization, a political appointee, was perceived as having more power than that of the director of the child welfare agency, both to influence the state's budget allocation to child welfare services as well as the nature of services in the state. The child welfare director, where this agency was part of an umbrella organization, was perceived as having less power, particularly over state budget allocations.

State-Local Relations — Local Autonomy and Monitoring of Local Agencies

The state agency formulates the rules and regulations that are implemented by the local agencies at the point of services delivery. The last two characteristics of the state agency studied were the degree of autonomy it allows to the local agencies and the extent to which it monitors the local agencies.

Two areas of local autonomy were explored — autonomy in defining risk to children and families, and autonomy in deciding the nature and timing of services to them. Fifteen states (44.1%) allowed medium level of autonomy. Another fifteen states (44.1%) leaned towards low autonomy and only four states (8.8%) were inclined towards high autonomy. The majority of the states allowed the same degree of autonomy in both areas of decisions — defining risk as well as the nature of services. In eleven states where there was some difference in the degree of autonomy in the two areas, a majority allowed greater autonomy in defining risk.

State monitoring of local agencies also varied but inclined towards close monitoring. Respondents were asked to specify the number and frequency of mechanisms used by the state agency to monitor their local agencies, and the mechanisms used by the state agency when a local agency was found to be out of compliance with state regulations. Two states reported no supervisory mechanisms to ensure compliance and no mechanisms when local agencies were out of compliance. One state used supervisory mechanisms only when needed. The majority of states used a combination of written reports, verbal reports, field visits, and quality control programs as supervisory mechanisms. Some states also reported use of automated computer data as a supervisory mechanism. When local agencies were found to be out of compliance, technical assistance, written and verbal reprimands were the most often used mechanisms. Three states took a punitive stance only (reprimands, sanctions, threat of reduction of funds) while four states took a more helpful stance only (technical assistance, financial assistance). Others used a combination of punitive and assistance-oriented mechanisms. A question was also asked about any state mechanisms to acknowledge, encourage, support or reward local agencies' success in preventing placement of children. Only six states (17.6%) responded in the affirmative. These mechanisms included verbal and written recognition to the local agency directly and in the state agency newsletter, and enhancement of funds to the local agency.

As discussed in the previous chapter, a scale of the variable monitoring, which ranged from 0 (no monitoring) to 95 (very high monitoring) was created by aggregating the states' scores on the number and frequency of supervisory mechanisms and the number of mechanisms used to assist local agencies' compliance. On this scale, eleven states scored in the low to medium range (10-29); five states scored in the medium range (30-39), and sixteen states scored in the medium to high range (40-69).

In summary, the state child welfare agency in most states was part of a large umbrella organization and was relatively highly placed in the state government structure. The director of this agency, usually appointed by the director of the umbrella organization, was perceived as having great influence on the nature of services in the state — the relative emphasis on primary prevention, preplacement prevention, reunification and permanency planning services. In most states this person could also influence, but to a lesser extent, the state budget allocations to child welfare services. The director of the umbrella organization was usually a governor appointee and had more power than the director of the child welfare agency in both areas of decisions. Most state agencies tended to allow a low to medium level of autonomy to their local service delivery agencies in deciding the nature and timing of the services and the population to be served, and they tended to monitor these local agencies from a medium to high level. Most state agencies used a combination of punitive and assistance-oriented mechanisms to ensure local agency compliance with state rules and regulations. Only six states had institutionalized tangible and intangible incentives for their local agencies to develop and strengthen prevention services.

States' Political and Ideological Environment

The state child welfare agency carries out its functions within the wider context of the state's political and ideological environment. Five indicators of the states' political and ideological environment were explored in this study: the states' history and tradition of child welfare services; their receptivity to federal direction; media attention to child welfare issues in the previous three years and its influence on services; support in legislature for traditional child welfare services (child protection, foster care and adoption); and support in legislature for primary prevention services.

History, Tradition and Receptivity to Federal Direction

Child welfare services have evolved differentially over the course of the states' history. Respondents were asked to describe their state in terms of its history of child welfare services, as a leader, as having an extensive history but not necessarily a leader, as having a history of average services, or as having provided minimal services historically. Thirteen states described themselves as leaders and eight states were described as having a history of extensive services. Thus, twenty-one states (61.8%) considered themselves leaders in child welfare services or had extensive history of child welfare services. Only two states were described as having a history of minimal child welfare services, while ten states considered themselves average.

Ten of the thirty-four respondent states had enacted child welfare legislation prior to 1980 that was similar in its intent to P.L. 96-272; some of these had served as models for P.L. 96-272. Eleven states enacted their child welfare legislation between 1981 and 1982. (P.L. 96-272 required prevention programs in place by 1 October 1982 to qualify for additional federal funds.) Apparently these states did not need major changes in their legislation to comply with the requirements of P.L. 96-272. Six states enacted their state laws after 1982, one being as recent as 1985. Two states did not have one single law but had amended statutes in other laws to qualify for federal foster care funds. One state responded that they did not have a companion law since P.L. 96-272 did not make such a requirement.

The state's historical relations with the federal government was examined to determine the extent to which it tended to be receptive to federal direction. Six states indicated they were highly receptive; twenty-three indicated they were somewhat receptive, while five indicated they were not receptive at all.

In terms of history and tradition thus, most states leaned towards a favorable history of child welfare services, and most states were receptive to federal direction. Only two states claimed to have a history of minimal services and little receptivity to federal direction. This perception is supported in states' timing of enactment of their current child welfare laws.

The Role of Media

The state's political and ideological environment is reflected in the issues covered by the public media. Respondents were asked to rate on a four-point scale the extent to which major newspapers and television in their state had carried stories on child protection, child abuse and neglect, foster care and adoption in the period 1982-85. They were then asked to rate the extent to which this media coverage was instrumental in bringing about changes in child welfare services in their state.

In thirty-two states (94.1%) public media had carried stories on child protection, foster care and adoption related issues; sixteen reported media coverage to a great extent while in the other sixteen there had been some media coverage. Only two states reported little or no media coverage. In sixteen states media coverage had strong influence and in nine states it had some influence in changes in primary prevention, preplacement prevention, reunification and permanency planning services. Thus, in almost three-fourths of the states media coverage was believed to have influenced child welfare services in the state.

Child welfare services, thus, were a public issue in a very large majority of states in this study. Media coverage of this issue seems to have been influential in bringing about changes in a full range of services to children and families, from primary prevention to permanency planning, in almost 75% of these states.

Support in State Legislature

The next set of questions solicited information on the extent to which the state's governor, legislators, state government officials, local government officials, and citizen groups had supported or lobbied for traditional child welfare services (child protection, foster care, adoption) and for primary prevention services in the period 1984-86. Respondents were asked to rate this support on a five-point scale, 1 denoting very strong support to 5 denoting opposition.

Governor's Support

A majority of the states enjoyed support from their governor, but the governors tended to support traditional child welfare services much more than primary prevention services. Of the thirty-two states that answered this question, governors in nineteen states (55.9%) supported traditional child welfare services strongly or very strongly, in seven (20.6%) states they supported them somewhat and six governors (17.6%) did not support them at all. Primary prevention services, on the other hand, were supported strongly or very strongly by only eight governors (23.5%), ten governors (29.4%) supported them somewhat and in nine states the governors (26.5%) did not support them at all. Thus, twenty-six state governors (76.5%) supported traditional child welfare services and eighteen state governors (52.9%) supported primary prevention services. Of these eighteen, five governors strongly supported both traditional and primary prevention services while three supported primary prevention more than traditional services. Seven state governors did not support either kind of service.

Legislative Support

Support from state legislators existed in a greater number of states, but with this group too support for traditional child welfare services was much higher than for primary prevention services. Eighteen states (52.9%) reported that their state legislators supported traditional services strongly or very strongly, thirteen (38.2%) reported some support and one reported no support. Primary prevention services were supported strongly or very strongly in eleven states (32.4%), had some support in fifteen (44.1%) states, and received no support in two states. Thus, legislative support for traditional child welfare services existed in thirty-one (91.2%) states and for primary prevention services in twenty-six (76.5%) states; but the intensity of support for primary prevention services was less. Five state legislatures strongly supported both kinds of services while two state legislatures supported primary prevention more than traditional services.

A comparison of governor's support and legislators' support indicated consensus between them in five states. In three states both the governor and members of the legislature supported both traditional and primary prevention services, in one state both groups did not support either kind of service and in one state both groups supported primary prevention more than traditional services. In twenty-seven states the governors and the legislators did not have a consensus on the nature of child welfare services to be provided in the state, but the disagreement was not strong enough to suggest possible conflict.

Internal Bureaucratic Support

The state and local government officials are most directly involved in service delivery, hence are most knowledgeable about the efficacy of the services provided. Respondents were asked to specify the state and local government officials who supported or lobbied for traditional child welfare services, and state and local government officials who supported or lobbied for primary prevention services in their state in the period 1984-86. In reporting this data, it is assumed that the officials specified expressed their support by lobbying.

At the state government level, six states (17.6%) reported very strong or strong support and six states (17.6%) reported some support for traditional child welfare services. The official most frequently identified was the director of the umbrella agency, whose support paralleled the governor's support. In two states the state attorney general was also reported to have supported traditional services. For primary prevention services, only three states (8.8%) reported strong to very strong support while eight states (8.8%) reported some support. In two states the state attorney general, and in one state the former child welfare director was identified as having strongly supported primary prevention services. While generally traditional services enjoyed support in a larger number of states, eight states reported state-level support for both traditional and primary prevention services while three states reported greater support for primary prevention than for traditional child welfare services.

Support from local government officials existed in two states only. The county directors supported primary prevention services strongly and traditional services somewhat, while the county commissioners and the mayors supported traditional services strongly and primary prevention services somewhat.

Citizen Support

As with state and local government officials, respondents were asked to specify the citizen groups and professional organizations that supported or lobbied for traditional child welfare services, and citizen and professional groups that supported or lobbied for primary prevention services in their state. In reporting this data, it is assumed that the groups specified expressed their support by lobbying.

Citizen and professional group support for traditional services existed in all states. In twenty-six (76.5%) states citizen groups supported primary prevention services also. While in no state did the citizen groups support primary prevention services more than traditional services, in twenty states (58.8%) there was equal support for both kinds of services. In a large number of states these groups could be clearly identified as providers, such as day care providers, residential treatment centers and group care providers. Some states reported support from citizen groups that could clearly be identified as consumers, such as the foster care association, adoptive parents groups, parents anonymous and the runaway network. Three states identified citizen groups that were clearly advocacy groups such as the Childrens' Defense Fund (one state) and the National Association of Social Workers (two states). However, several states specified numerous groups that could not be so easily categorized, such as the Child Abuse Consortium, Childrens' Alliance, Task Force on Children and the Network for Children.

These groups could be coalitions of advocates, providers and consumers. In one state the medical association also lobbied for traditional child welfare services. Two states reported both opposition and support from citizen groups, children's advocates lobbying for traditional as well as primary prevention services and the family rights groups opposing them both. In one state a strong controversy was generated after high media exposure of the death of a child returned to the family by the local child protective services, with both sides wanting change. This public debate led to the appointment of a Governor's Task Force which eventually influenced some change in services.

In summary, citizen support was found to exist in all states and the level of support from citizen groups was found to be much higher than from the state governments, that is, the governor, the legislature, and the state and local government officials. This was true for traditional child welfare services as well as for primary prevention services.

Index of Political and Ideological Environment

An index of political and ideological environment was created by aggregating the strong and very strong scores for each state on each of the indicators discussed above. Possible scores on this index ranged from 0 which indicated a highly unfavorable environment to 28 which indicated a highly favorable environment in which the state had a very favorable history of child welfare services, was very receptive to federal direction, had a high media coverage and high influence of this coverage on services, and enjoyed strong or very strong support for both traditional child welfare services and primary prevention services from the state governor, the legislature, state and local government officials and citizen groups. On this index, scores for the thirty-four states in this study ranged from 1 to 18. Four states scored between 1 and 4; seven states scored between 6 and 7; eight states scored between 8 and 10; seven states scored between 11 and 13 and eight states scored between 14 and 18.

In summary, the political and ideological climate of the states varied. Fifteen states had a favorable environment for child welfare services, eight being very favorable and seven as somewhat favorable. On the other end, nineteen states had unfavorable environment, eleven being very unfavorable and eight somewhat unfavorable. Child welfare services was a public issue in all but two states in this study as evidenced by the stories carried in public media. Generally, there was much greater support for traditional child welfare services, that is, child protection, foster care and adoption services, than for primary prevention services for all families. Support was also much greater from citizen groups — providers, consumers and advocates of services than from the state governments, including the governors, state legislatures, and state and local government officials. Only about half the state governors supported these services, and support from state directors, generally appointed by the governors, paralleled the governors' position. A greater number of state legislatures supported these services. In twenty-seven states, differences existed between the governors' and the state legislators' support, but the differences were not strong enough to suggest conflict between them.

Primary prevention services were also an issue in states. In almost 60% of the states, citizen groups lobbied for primary prevention services as much as for traditional services. In some states the governors, the legislators and other officials also supported primary prevention services as much as traditional services, and in a few states these people lobbied for primary prevention more than for traditional services.

Disposition of Implementors

Implementors will implement a policy to the extent they agree with its objectives and its underlying social values. Furthermore, the intensity of implementors' agreement or disagreement may also affect the implementation process; those holding intense negative orientations towards the policy may openly defy program objectives while persons with less intense attitude may attempt surreptitious diversion and evasion.

The objectives of P.L. 96-272 are based on the value of a permanent family, preferably the biological family, for each child. This Act, for the first time in American history, establishes government's responsibility to support, maintain and preserve the biological family (aside from income maintenance) and to provide an alternate permanent family to the child if the biological family cannot provide adequate care. The state level implementors who translate these social values into services are the state governor, the key legislator, the director of the state child welfare agency, and the director of the umbrella organization when the state child welfare agency was part of an umbrella organization.

In this study's questionnaire, these social values were presented in the form of four statements. First, "the biological family is most important in care and upbringing of children; family ties should not be broken unless child's physical safety is at risk." Second, "if parents cannot provide adequate care to their children, it is the responsibility of the government to help them do so." Third, "government should not wait till a family becomes dysfunctional to provide help; comprehensive social services should be available to all families so that they do not become dysfunctional." And fourth, "if a family cannot care for its children even with help, then it is the responsibility of the government to find alternate permanent families for the children." Respondents were asked to rate, on a four-point scale which extended from 1 (strong agreement) to 4 (strong disagreement), the extent to which they believed the four implementors described above in their state agreed or disagreed with each of these four statements.

Agreement with the first statement, the importance of the biological family, was unanimous. In the states that responded to this set of questions, 86.7% of the governors and state agency directors, and 75.0% of the key legislators were perceived as strongly agreeing with this statement; nobody disagreed (see Table 6a).

Table 6a
Implementors' Agreement With Statement 1

Statement 1 — The biological family is most important in care and upbringing of children; family ties should not be broken unless child's physical safety is at risk.

	Strongly agree f (%)	Agree f (%)	Disagree f (%)	Strongly disagree f (%)	Totals f (%)
Governor	26 (86.7)	4 (13.3)	0	0	30 (100)
Key legislator	24 (75.0)	8 (25.0)	0	0	32 (100)
Umbrella agency director	26 (86.7)	4 (13.3)	0	0	30 (100)
Child welfare director	26 (86.7)	4 (13.3)	0	0	30 (100)

The intensity of agreement with the idea of governmental responsibility reduced successively as it moved from responsibility for children to responsibility for families. The child welfare directors were perceived in most states as strongly agreeing with all four statements. But fewer respondents perceived their state's governor, the key legislator and the director of the umbrella organization as strongly agreeing with the notion of governmental responsibility for finding alternate permanent families for children. In a few states all four implementors were perceived as disagreeing with this statement (see Table 6b).

Table 6b
Implementors' Agreement With Statement 4

Statement 4 — If a family cannot care for its children even with help, then it is the responsibility of the government to find alternate permanent families for the children.

	Strongly agree f (%)	Agree f (%)	Disagree f (%)	Strongly disagree f (%)	Totals f (%)
Governor	17 (53.1)	12 (37.5)	3 (9.4)	0	32 (100)
Key legislator	19 (59.4)	11 (34.4)	2 (6.2)	0	32 (100)
Umbrella agency director	20 (66.7)	8 (26.7)	2 (6.7)	0	30 (100.1)
Child welfare director	26 (96.7)	2 (6.7)	2 (6.7)	0	30 (100.1)

Even fewer respondents perceived the governor, the key legislator, and the director of umbrella organization as strongly agreeing with the notion of governmental responsibility to help families when they could not care for their children. In two states they were perceived as disagreeing, and in one state they were perceived as strongly disagreeing (see Table 6c).

Table 6c
Implementors' Agreement With Statement 2

Statement 2 — If parents cannot provide adequate care to their children, it is the responsibility of the government to help them do so.

	Strongly agree f (%)	Agree f (%)	Disagree f (%)	Strongly disagree f (%)	Totals f (%)
Governor	12 (37.5)	17 (53.1)	2 (6.2)	1 (3.1)	32 (99.9)
Key legislator	11 (34.4)	18 (56.3)	2 (6.2)	1 (3.1)	32 (100)
Umbrella agency director	15 (50.0)	12 (40.0)	2 (6.7)	1 (3.3)	30 (100)
Child welfare director	20 (66.7)	8 (26.7)	0	2 (6.7)	30 (100.1)

The number of states where the governor, the key legislator, and the director of the umbrella organization were perceived as strongly agreeing with the third statement referring to the responsibility of the government to provide primary prevention services to all families was sharply reduced. More implementors disagreed, and one umbrella agency director was perceived as strongly disagreeing with this statement (see Table 6d).

Table 6d
Implementors' Agreement With Statement 3

Statement 3 — Government should not wait until a family becomes dysfunctional to provide help; comprehensive social services should be available to all families so that they do not become dysfunctional.

	Strongly agree f (%)	Agree f (%)	Disagree f (%)	Strongly disagree f (%)	Totals f (%)
Governor	9 (28.1)	20 (62.5)	3 (9.4)	0	32 (100)
Key legislator	9 (28.1)	18 (56.3)	5 (15.6)	0	32 (100)
Umbrella agency director	12 (40.0)	16 (53.3)	1 (3.3)	1 (3.3)	30 (99.9)
Child welfare director	23 (76.7)	7 (23.3)	0	0	30 (100)

An index of disposition of implementors was created by aggregating the score of each implementor on each of the four statements. Possible scores on this index ranged from 4, indicating strong agreement with all four statements to 16, indicating strong disagreement with all four statements. On this index, state governors ranged between 4 and 9 with a mean score of 6.25 and standard deviation of 2.66; the key legislators ranged between 4 and 9 with a mean score of 6.31 and standard deviation of 1.73; the umbrella agency directors ranged between 4 and 10 with a mean score of 5.96 and standard deviation of 1.56; and the child welfare directors ranged between 4 and 8 with a mean score of 4.97 and standard deviation of 1.23.

In summary, the child welfare directors in a large majority of responding states were perceived as strongly agreeing with the social values underlying P.L. 96-272. The state governors, the key legislators, and the directors of the umbrella organizations where the child welfare agency was part of an umbrella organization were perceived as agreeing with the importance of the biological family in all states, and agreeing to a lesser extent with the notion of governmental responsibility to find alternate

permanent homes for children in a majority of states. However, the intensity
of their agreement with the idea of governmental responsibility to help
families was much less. On an index of disposition which ranged from 4
indicating strong agreement to 16 indicating strong disagreement with the
values inherent in P.L. 96-272, the governors' average score was 6.25; the key
legislators averaged 6.31; the umbrella agency directors averaged 5.96 and
the child welfare directors averaged 4.97.

States' Social and Economic Conditions

The social and economic conditions of the states relevant to this study
were their need for child welfare services and the economic resources
available to them to provide these services. Data on states' nonwhite child
population was also gathered to explore its effect on the provision of child
welfare services.

Need

In this study, five indicators of states' need were measured. The three
direct indicators were the proportion of child population in the states,
proportion of children in out-of-home care and the proportion of children
involved in reports of suspected neglect or abuse. The two indirect indicators
were the proportion of children living below the state's poverty level and
the proportion of children living in single-parent families.

Characteristics of Children

According to the 1980 census, children below 18 years of age in the
study states ranged from 145,318 to over 6.3 million. Ranging between 24%
and 37%, the states' child population averaged 28.9% (standard deviation
2.4). Of this total child population, the nonwhite child population (Black,
Spanish origin and Asian children) ranged between less than 1% in three
states to 21% in one state, with an average of 5.9% (standard deviation 3.28).

Data for children in out-of-home care in 1985 were available for
twenty-seven states only. Ranging from less than 1% to 3% of the states'
child population, children in out-of-home care averaged 0.6% (standard
deviation 0.5). In seventeen of these twenty-seven states, children in
out-of-home care comprised between 0.17% to 0.67% of their total child
population. In nine states 1% and in one state 3% of its' child population was
in out-of-home care.

Data for children involved in reports of suspected neglect or abuse in 1985 were available for all thirty-four states. In two states only 1% of the child population, in twenty-seven states 2-4% of their child population, and in three states 6% of their child population was involved in reports of suspected neglect or abuse. On an average, 3.2% of the states' child population was involved in reports of suspected abuse or neglect (standard deviation 1.2).

A much higher proportion of children were living below the state's poverty level and in single-parent families. According to the 1980 census, in one state as few as 2% of its children, and in another state as many as 51% of its children lived below the poverty level. Comprising between 10% and 15% of the child population in nineteen states and between 15% and 23% of the child population in nine states, children living below the state's poverty level averaged 16.3% (standard deviation 8.2). Children living in single-parent families, on the other hand, ranged from 4% of the child population in one state to 22% of the child population in another state. Constituting between 15% and 19% of the state's child population in twenty-two states in this study, child population living in single-parent families averaged 15.4% (standard deviation 3.7).

As discussed in the previous chapter, an index to measure the relative need of the states was constructed by aggregating the percent of child population involved in reports of suspected neglect or abuse, living below the poverty level and living in single-parent families in each state. On this index of possible scores between 0 and 100, states ranged between 19 (one state) and 68 (one state). Eight states scored between 20 and 28, sixteen states scored between 30 and 39, seven states scored between 40 and 48, and one state scored 51.

In summary, children constituted from 24% to 37% of the states' total population in 1980, of which between 1% and 21% were nonwhite. Of this child population, in most states between 2% and 4% were involved in reports of child abuse or neglect, and in most states 1% or less of their child population was in out-of-home care. Thus, if need is defined on the basis of proportion of children in out-of-home care or proportion of children identified to be at risk through a report of suspected abuse or neglect, then need in states for child welfare services does not appear to be very high. However, if need is defined on the basis of proportion of children at risk for child abuse or neglect, then a different picture emerges. The population most at risk, children living below the poverty level ranged from 2% in one state to 51% in one state. In most states this population ranged from 10% to 23% with an average of 16.3%. Children living in single-parent families ranged from 4% to 22%; in most states this population ranged from 15% to 19% with an average of 15.4%. On an index of relative need which extended from 0 (no need) to 100 (desperate need), states ranged between 19 and 68, with almost half the states falling in the 30-39 range.

Resources

In this study, the variable "resources" was measured as per capita revenue of the state in the year 1985. States' economic resources derived primarily from two sources, the intergovernmental funds from federal and local governments, and state taxes. Intergovernmental revenue was found to have derived primarily from the federal government; in most states the revenue from the local governments formed a very small proportion of the total intergovernmental funds. Most states levied taxes on individual income, and business and corporate income; most states also levied sales tax, property tax and death and gift tax. Some funds were also received from licensing fees and from interest income. States' total revenues were expended on nine major items; these included highways, police, corrections (adult and youth), education, hospitals, health and mental health care, salaries and wages, public welfare, and interest on general debt. Public welfare programs included social services, social insurance (OASDI, SSI, Medicare and Medicaid) and public assistance programs such as AFDC, food stamps, general relief and Refugee Cash Assistance Program.

The total per capita revenue of states ranged from $1214 to $3822, with an average of $1879 (standard deviation 528.91). In most states, however, it tended to be towards the lower rather than the higher end of the range. Eleven states received between $1200 and $1600, ten states received between $1600 and $2000 and eight states received between $2000 and $2300 per capita. In two states the per capita revenue ranged between $2450 and $2700 and in only one state it was as high as $3822. In half the states in this study the per capita revenue was below $1729.

States collected much higher revenue from their taxes than from the federal government. Revenue from the federal government ranged between $207 and $831 and averaged $375.38 (standard deviation $116.48). Two states received $580 and $831 per capita respectively; all the other states received less than $550 per capita from the federal government. Half the states in this study received between $264 and $384. Revenue from state taxes, on the other hand, ranged from $435 to $1584, with an average of $853.94 (standard deviation 231.83). Twenty-four states collected between $600 and $925 per capita in taxes. Two states clearly emerged as low tax states, collecting $435 and about $500 per capita, while five states clearly emerged as higher tax states, collecting about $1000, $1150, $1250 and $1584 per capita respectively.

In summary, states' economic resources measured as per capita revenue ranged from $1214 to $3822, but in majority of the states this was below $2000. Per capita revenue from state taxes was more than twice the amount of per capita revenue from federal government. The total revenue was expended on nine major items; these included highways, police, corrections (adult and youth), education, hospitals, health and mental health care, salaries and wages, public welfare, and interest on general debt. The major categories of public welfare expenditures were social insurance programs such as Unemployment and Disability Insurance, Supplemental Security Income, Medicare and Medicaid; and public assistance programs such as Aid to Families with Dependent Children, Food Stamps, General Relief and Refugee Cash Assistance Program.

C. Changes Since P.L. 96-272

In the last ten years, some changes have obviously occurred in the social conditions that form the wider context of child and family welfare services. Nationally in 1985, the number of children in out-of-home care had decreased by 17.7% since 1978. As compared to 1980, the number of children involved in reports of neglect and abuse had increased by 67.7%. Child welfare expenditures had also increased by 1.7%, but when adjusted for inflation, they had decreased by 7.8%. In this part, changes in the nature and scope of child welfare services and in the designated child welfare agencies in the study states are described. Significance of this Act as an incentive for these changes, as perceived by the respondents, is also described.

Changes in Services

There has been an increase in both the strength of services and the number of states providing all four kinds of child welfare services. This increase has occurred most notably in the area of primary prevention services.

Primary prevention services existed in at least half the counties of nineteen (55.9%) states in 1978-79; in 1985-86 they existed in at least half the counties of twenty-eight states (82.3%). Preplacement prevention services existed in thirty-one (91.2%) states in 1978-79; in 1985-86 they existed in thirty-three (97.0%) states. Similarly, reunification and permanency planning services existed in atleast half the counties of thirty (88.2%) states each in 1978-79; in 1985-86 they existed in all (100%) the states in this study[3].

In a majority of the states where they existed prior to 1980, all these services were strengthened and increased, but in two states the primary and preplacement prevention services were decreased. One of these states is a leader in child welfare services; it had passed its child welfare law, incorporating all the aspects of prevention prior to P.L. 96-272. Respondent from this state commented: "The reduction of six million federal dollars in Title XX Block Grant and no state match requirements had a major negative impact on child welfare services in our state. This coupled with Gramm-Rudman cuts and the state downturn in economy further reduced funding so that increasingly the focus is on crisis intervention and short-term efforts. Reduction of prevention services also occurred..."

Indeed this movement towards crisis intervention and short-term services was observed in the other states also. Crisis intervention services, that is services delivered for up to one month only, increased in twenty-seven (79.4%) states and decreased in only two (5.9%) states. Short-term services, that is, services delivered for up to six months increased in twenty-nine (85.3%) states and decreased in two (5.9%) states. Long-term services, that is, services delivered for up to two years increased in twenty (58.8%) states and decreased in eight (23.5%) states; whereas services with no time limit increased in sixteen (47.1%) states and decreased in twelve (35.3%) states.

Changes in Agencies

Derthick (1970), in her analysis of federal influence through the grant system, hypothesizes that federal grants strengthen the power of the implementing agency in the state. A set of questions was included in the study questionnaire to explore changes in the states' implementing agencies in the wake of enactment of P.L. 96-272.

Most states reported little or no change in most aspects of their child welfare agencies. At the state level, the state agency budget had increased in 65.6% states and the size of its staff had increased in 56.3% states. The status of the state agency remained unchanged in 68.8% of the states but was elevated in the remaining 31.2% states. The director's power remained unchanged in 71.9% states but was reported to have decreased in three (9.4%) states. The ability of the child welfare advocates in the state to influence the increase in programs increased in 56.2% states, and their ability to halt or reduce the rate of cutbacks increased in 28.1% states.

In terms of the local agencies' capacity to provide services, the most notable increases were in the size of direct service staff (54.8% states) and in caseloads of the direct service staff (58.6% states). Local autonomy had not changed in half the states; in the remaining states half reported increase while the other half reported a decrease.

Perception of Incentive

Respondents were asked to rate the significance of P.L. 96-272 as an incentive in bringing about the increase in services. To be more specific in the questionnaire, the "carrot" aspect of P.L. 96-272 was presented in the form of two phrases, "increase in federal funds" and "potential of increase in federal funds," and the "stick" aspect was presented in the form of two phrases, "potential of loss of federal funds" and "potential of restriction of federal funds." Respondents were asked to indicate the extent these "carrots" and "sticks" had played a role in increasing various kinds of child welfare service by rating each as very significant, somewhat significant, and as having little or no significance.

For increase in primary prevention services, the twenty-seven states that answered this question were divided in their perception of the carrots as significant; in thirteen states the increase or potential of increase of federal funds was perceived as significant, in fourteen states it was perceived as having little or no significance. The stick — possible loss of federal funds — was perceived as significant in a somewhat higher number of states (see Table 7a).

Table 7a
Significance of P.L. 96-272 in Increasing Primary Prevention Services

	Very significant f (%)	Somewhat significant f (%)	Little or no significance f (%)	Totals f (%)
Increase in federal funds	6 (22.2)	7 (25.9)	14 (51.9)	27 (100)
Potential of increase in federal funds	4 (14.8)	9 (33.3)	14 (51.9)	27 (100)
Potential of loss of federal funds	8 (29.6)	8 (29.6)	11 (40.8)	27 (99.9)
Potential of restriction of federal funds	5 (19.2)	7 (26.9)	15 (53.8)	26 (99.9)

For preplacement prevention services the sticks were perceived as significant by a greater number of states, whereas they were divided in their perception of the carrots as significant incentive. Twenty-two out of thirty states (73.3%) perceived the potential of loss of federal funds, and nineteen out of twenty-eight states (67.8%) perceived the potential of restriction of federal funds as having had a significant influence. Almost 60% of the states perceived the increase in federal funds as significant (see Table 7b).

Table 7b
Significance of P.L. 96-272 in Increasing Preplacement Prevention Services

	Very significant f (%)	Somewhat significant f (%)	Little or no significance f (%)	Totals f (%)
Increase in federal funds	7 (25.9)	9 (33.3)	11 (40.7)	27 (99.9)
Potential of increase in federal funds	7 (26.9)	6 (23.1)	13 (50.0)	26 (100)
Potential of loss of federal funds	13 (43.3)	9 (30.0)	8 (26.7)	30 (100)
Potential of restriction of federal funds	6 (21.4)	13 (46.4)	9 (32.1)	28 (99.9)

For reunification services both the carrot and the stick were perceived as significant. The incentive, however, was the actual rather than the potential increase in federal funds, which is likely to have increased the states' capacity to provide these services. The stick was the potential loss, not the restriction of federal funds (see Table 7c).

Table 7c Significance of P.L. 96-272 in Increasing Reunification Services				
	Very significant f (%)	Somewhat significant f (%)	Little or no significance f (%)	Totals f (%)
Increase in federal funds	8 (26.7)	9 (30.0)	13 (43.3)	30 (100)
Potential of increase in federal funds	8 (29.6)	6 (22.2)	13 (48.2)	27 (100)
Potential of loss of federal funds	14 (45.2)	8 (25.8)	9 (29.0)	31 (100)
Potential of restriction of federal funds	8 (28.6)	11 (39.3)	9 (32.1)	28 (100)

For permanency planning services both the carrots — actual and potential increase of federal funds, and the sticks — potential of loss or restriction of funds — were perceived as significant by a large majority of states (see Table 7d).

Table 7d Significance of P.L. 96-272 in Increasing Permanency Planning Services				
	Very significant f (%)	Somewhat significant f (%)	Little or no significance f (%)	Totals f (%)
Increase in federal funds	11 (36.7)	9 (30.0)	10 (33.3)	30 (100)
Potential of increase in federal funds	7 (25.9)	8 (29.6)	12 (44.4)	27 (99.9)
Potential of loss of federal funds	13 (41.9)	9 (29.0)	9 (29.0)	31 (99.9)
Potential of restriction of federal funds	6 (22.2)	12 (44.4)	9 (33.3)	27 (99.9)

Thus, while states were divided in their perception of the significance of P.L. 96-272 in the increase of primary prevention services, it was perceived as significant in the increases in all the other kinds of child welfare services in the states in this study. For services for which federal funds were forthcoming, such as reunification and particularly permanency planning, both the carrot and the stick aspects, the actual increase in funds and the potential of loss or restriction of funds were perceived as significant. For primary prevention services the intended federal funds had not been forthcoming but the penalties were often perceived to exist, whether or not enforced. These penalties, the threat of loss of funds, was perceived as significant incentive by about three-fourths of the respondents.

These findings suggest that there would have been far greater development of preventive services, that indeed most states were philosophically prepared to do so, had the intended federal funds been available. Respondent from one state comments: "P.L. 96-272 has had a great effect on staff training, attitudes about permanency planning and family reunification, but because of declining state and federal budgets and need for economic restraints it has probably not had as large an effect as intended. We 'believe' in all the intents of the law but often do not have the dollars to make needed changes, support prevention activities etc. Federal dollars do not seem to be driving services towards prevention at this time — amount of money isn't enough to accomplish that end." This respondent could very well be voicing the experience of most states.

In summary, P.L. 96-272 has had a mixed effect on states' child welfare systems and services. It was perceived by a majority of states as an incentive for increases in services. For services for which federal funds were made available, such as permanency planning and reunification services, both the carrot and the stick aspects of the Act were perceived as incentives. For prevention services the expected federal funds had not been forthcoming; states were divided in their perception of increase in federal funds as incentive but a larger number of states perceived the threat of reduction of federal funds as an incentive. States were divided in the extent to which the ability of their child welfare advocates had been strengthened in the wake of this Act. The size of staff had increased both at state and local levels, but the states were divided in the extent to which the power of the state agency or the service delivery capacity of the local agencies had changed.

Summary

States' expenditure per child on child welfare and their prevention effort varied widely. A comparison of states' relative emphasis on the four kinds of child welfare services indicates the greatest emphasis on preplacement prevention and reunification services and the least emphasis on primary prevention services. Child welfare services were primarily a federal-state program with little local fiscal participation, and they comprised a very minor part of the total state expenditures.

State laws governing child welfare services generally did not provide clear guidelines for implementing preventive services. In most states these services were not mandated, few of those mandating them provided additional resources, and professional competence of service delivery staff was rarely mandated. In majority of states the designated state child welfare agency was part of a large umbrella organization and was relatively highly placed in the state government structure. Both the director of the child welfare agency and the director of the umbrella organization were perceived as having had considerable power in the state government, both to influence the state budgetary process and to influence the nature of services in the state. In most states the state agency allowed low to medium level of autonomy to the local agencies and monitored the local agencies from a medium to high level.

Child welfare was a public issue in all but two states in this study, but in more than half the states the political and ideological environment was not favorable for child welfare services. In the states' legislature in 1985, traditional child welfare services, that is child protection, foster care, and adoption enjoyed much more support than primary prevention services. But support from citizen and professional groups for both traditional services and for primary prevention services far outnumbered the support from individuals in the states' governments. The child welfare directors in a majority of states were perceived as strongly agreeing with the social values embodied in P.L. 96-272. The governors, the key legislators, and the directors of the umbrella agency were perceived as agreeing with the notion of importance of the biological family for the child, but the intensity of their agreement decreased as the notion moved from government responsibility for children to government responsibility for all families.

States' need for child welfare services, if defined as proportion of its child population and proportion of children in out-of-home care, does not appear to be very high. But if defined as proportion of children at risk of out-of-home placement, then on a scale of 0 to 100 need ranged from 19 to 68, with majority of states ranging between 30 and 39. States collected more than twice as much per capita revenue from their taxes than from the federal government. In most states the total revenue was expended on nine major categories of expenditure, which included highways, police, corrections, education, health care, salaries and wages, public welfare and interest on general debt.

Both the number of states providing all four kinds of services and the strength of these services had increased since the enactment of P.L. 96-272. Notably about 26% more states were providing some primary prevention services in at least half the counties of their state in 1985. The trend, however was towards emergency and short-term services. P.L. 96-272 was perceived in most states as incentive for increase in services. For permanency planning services for which federal funds were available, both the increase in funds and the threat of loss or restriction of funds were perceived as incentives. For prevention services for which federal funds were not forthcoming, states were divided in their perception of the carrot aspect of P.L. 96-272 as an incentive but a somewhat higher number of states perceived the stick aspect, potential of loss of federal funds, as an incentive.

From their comments it appears more states were philosophically prepared to provide more prevention services, but cuts in Title XX funds, elimination of the state match requirements, and a general downturn in states' economy imposed severe budgetary constraints. In one state that considers itself historically a leader in child welfare services, prevention services had to be reduced for these reasons. One cannot help but believe that had the intended federal funds been available, states would have made far more gains in the direction of prevention.

V
Findings — Relationships Between Variables

In this chapter, associations between the two dependent variables (expenditure per child and prevention effort) and the four independent variables are discussed. As all variables were measured at interval or ratio level, Pearson's correlation coefficient is used to test associations and hypotheses. Multiple regression analysis was conducted with variables found to have high correlation with the two dependent variables. A .05 level of significance is used; however, because of the small size of the sample, attention is also drawn to statistical significance of associations at an extended level of .10. All correlations above the .10 level are considered not significant.

This study was based on the propositions that variations existed between states in their child welfare expenditures and prevention effort; and, that states did not perceive P.L. 96-272 as incentive for development of primary prevention services. As discussed in the previous chapter, child welfare expenditures in the states in this study were found to range from $2.71 to $197.65 per child. This being univariate data, a statistical test of significance could not be done, but a visual examination of this data reported in Table 1 (Chapter IV) supports the proposition of variation in child welfare expenditures. Similarly, states' prevention effort was found to vary from 15% to 75% of staff time on prevention services. A statistical test of significance could not be done, but a visual examination of this data also supports this proposition (see Table 4, Chapter IV). The third proposition, also univariate data, was not supported by visual examination. States were found to be divided in their perception of significance of P.L. 96-272 in the development of primary prevention services. Of the twenty-seven states that answered this set of questions, almost half perceived the fiscal incentives and penalties as significant or very significant; a little over half the states perceived them as having had little significance (see Table 7a, Chapter IV). A statistical test of significance could not be done as the categories in this table are not mutually exclusive. Descriptive comments from some respondents indicated that P.L. 96-272 had been effective in changing the attitudes of staff and in inculcating belief in permanency planning philosophy, but that states were unable to implement preventive services because of financial constraints.

Expenditure Per Child and Prevention Effort

States' expenditure per child on child welfare services was found to be significantly associated with the proportion of federal contribution to states' child welfare expenditures (r = .3983, p < .013). Proportion of state contribution was also found to be significantly associated with expenditure per child (r = .3642, p < .024). No significant association was found between local contribution and expenditure per child (r = .2039, NS).

One would expect that higher expenditure per child would imply higher prevention effort in the states. This was not found to be true; states' expenditure per child was not significantly associated with their prevention effort (r = .02; NS). However, proportion of federal contribution was associated with prevention effort (r = .2786, p < .065). A scattergram of these two variables indicates a positive linear relationship; as the federal contribution increased from 37% to 80%, in the twelve states in this range prevention effort increased from 15% to 40%. The distribution was random below 37% and above 80%. No significant association was found between prevention effort and proportion of state contribution (r = .144, NS) or between prevention effort and proportion of local contribution (r = .2786, NS).

Testing Hypotheses — Bivariate Analysis

Van Horn and Van Meter's model of intergovernmental policy implementation that forms the theoretical guide to this study identifies eight variable clusters and relationships among them. Two of these clusters relate to the nature of the policy — the adequacy and timing of resources, and the clarity, consistency and accuracy of standards and objectives. They refer to the other six clusters as "linkages". These include communication, enforcement, political conditions (the extent of support or opposition in public and elite opinion), characteristics of the implementing agency, disposition of the implementors, and social and economic conditions (needs and resources). In the implementation of P.L. 96-272 the reduction of resources, lack of standards and enforcement by the federal government, and communication from the federal administration of its wish to repeal this Act were discussed in Chapter II. This study explored the role of the remaining four linkage variables, hypothesizing that the variation in states' child welfare expenditure and prevention effort was related to the characteristics of the designated child welfare agency, states' political and ideological environment, disposition of state-level implementors, and states' social and economic conditions. Bivariate analyses were conducted to test each of these hypotheses.

> *Hypothesis 1. Variation in states' child welfare expenditures and prevention effort was related to characteristics of implementing agency , its structure and status in the state government.*

As discussed in the previous chapter, five characteristics of the state's designated child welfare agency were measured. These included its status in the state government, its size, powers of the directors of the child welfare agency and the umbrella agency when the child welfare agency was part of an umbrella organization, the extent of autonomy the state agency allowed to the local agencies, and the extent the state agency monitored the local agencies. The relationship between each of these characteristics with expenditure per child and with prevention effort was tested.

Expenditure Per Child

Of the five characteristics of the state child welfare system, only the status of the state agency was found to have a significant association with per child expenditure ($r = .3181$, $p < .046$). In other words, no significant association was found between per child expenditure and size of the agency ($r = .0188$; NS); power of the director of umbrella agency ($r = .1383$, NS) or power of the director of the child welfare agency ($r = .1304$, NS). No significant association was found between per child expenditure and the extent of monitoring ($r = .0097$, NS); or the degree of local autonomy ($r = .2084$, NS).

Prevention Effort

No significant association was found between prevention effort and any characteristics of the implementing agency (status: $r = -.2114$; size: $r = -.0088$; power, director umbrella agency: $r = -.0817$; power, director child welfare agency: $r = -.0776$; monitoring: $r = -.0097$; autonomy: $r = .1718$).

In summary, the only characteristic of the state child welfare agency found to have a statistically significant association with states' per child expenditure on child welfare services was its status in the state government structure. But neither this nor any other characteristic was found to be significantly associated with prevention effort.

Hypothesis 2. Variation in states' child welfare expenditures and prevention effort was related to its political and ideological environment.

The nature of the political and ideological environment was measured as a composite index of thirteen subvariables. These included the state's history of child welfare services, its receptivity to federal direction, media exposure to child welfare related issues in the previous three years, support in state legislature for traditional child welfare services from the state governor, key legislator, state government officials, local government officials and citizen groups, and support in state legislature for primary prevention services from the state governor, key legislator, state government officials, local government officials and citizen groups.

Expenditure Per Child

As a composite index, the states' political and ideological environment was not significantly correlated with their expenditure per child on child welfare services (r = -.0156, NS). Further analysis was done to explore associations between expenditure per child and any of the subvariables that comprised this index; none was found. The correlational values, none of which were statistically significant, were: history: r = -.0860; receptivity to federal direction: r = -.0718; media exposure: r = .0179; support for traditional child welfare services: governor: r = .0695 ; legislature: r = .1595; state government officials: r = .0562; citizen groups: r = -.0926. Support for primary prevention services: governor, r = -.0339; legislature, r = -.2028; state government officials, r = -.5408; citizen groups, r = -.0606. Not enough cases existed to test correlation between the local government officials' support and child welfare expenditures.

Prevention Effort

Nor was prevention effort significantly associated with states' political and ideological environment as measured on the composite index (r = .0406, NS). Further analysis of association between prevention effort and each of the subvariables comprising this index revealed significant association with support from citizen groups for traditional services (r = .5413, p < .0001) and state government officials' support for traditional child welfare services (r = 7217, p < .053). Support of these two groups for primary prevention services, however, was not significantly associated with prevention effort (citizen support for primary prevention services, r = .1214, NS; state officials' support for primary prevention services, r = .7251, NS). Prevention effort was associated with support for primary prevention services from members of the states' legislatures at .1 level (r = .2740, p < .079). No significant association was found between prevention effort and the remaining subvariables. The correlational values were: history: r = .0080; receptivity to federal direction: r = -.1571; media exposure: r = .0492. Support for traditional child welfare services: governor, r = -.0491 ; legislature, r = .1974. Support for primary prevention services: governor, r = .2175; state government officials, r = .2751. Not enough cases of support of local government officials existed to test association with prevention effort.

In summary, as a composite index of thirteen subvariables the states' political and ideological environment was not significantly associated with either the states' expenditure per child or their prevention effort. On further analysis, none of the thirteen subvariables separately were found to have a significant association with expenditure per child, but support of citizen groups and state government officials for traditional child welfare services was associated with prevention effort at .05 level of significance, and support of states' legislators for primary prevention services was associated with prevention effort at .1 level of significance.

> *Hypothesis 3. Variation in child welfare expenditures and prevention effort was related to the disposition of major implementors.*

Disposition of the implementors was measured as the extent to which they agreed or disagreed with the social values underlying P.L. 96-272—the importance of the biological family for the child, the responsibility of government to provide services to families to prevent unnecessary separation of children and to find alternate permanent families for children when biological families cannot provide adequate care, and to provide primary prevention services to all families. The state-level implementors were identified as the governor, the key legislator, the director of the state child welfare agency, and the director of the umbrella organization when the state agency was part of an umbrella organization. A composite score for the disposition of each implementor was computed by aggregating the score on each of these values; a score of 4 thus denoted very favorable disposition and a score of 16 denoted very unfavorable disposition.

Dispositions of none of the four implementors were found to be significantly associated with expenditure per child (governor: $r = -.0388$; key legislator: $r = -.1437$; director of the umbrella agency: $r = .0990$; director of the child welfare agency: $r = -.1055$). However, dispositions of the governor, the key legislator, and the director of the child welfare agency were found to be significantly associated with prevention effort (governor, $r = -.3602$, $p < .021$; key legislator, $r = -.3071$, $p < .044$; director, child welfare agency, $r = -.3243$, $p < .043$). Disposition of the director of the umbrella agency was not significantly associated with prevention effort ($r = -.1341$, NS).

In summary, disposition of implementors — the extent to which they agreed with the values of permanency planning philosophy — was not significantly associated with states' child welfare expenditure. But, the dispositions of the governor, the key legislator, and the director of the child welfare agency were found to be significantly associated with prevention effort.

> *Hypothesis 4. Variation in states' child welfare expenditures and prevention effort was related to its social and economic conditions (need, resources, and nonwhite child population).*

Need and Expenditure Per Child

As discussed in the previous chapter, five indicators of need were measured in this study. These included the proportion of child population in the states; proportion of children in out-of-home care; proportion of children involved in reports of suspected abuse or neglect; proportion of children living below the state's poverty level; and proportion of children living in single-parent families. No associations were found at .05 level of significance. At .1 level the proportion of states' child population ($r = .2524$, $p < .075$) and proportion of children in single-parent families ($r = .2417$, $p < .084$) were associated with expenditure per child. No significant association was found with proportion of children living in out-of-home care ($r = .0836$, NS); proportion of children involved in reports of abuse or neglect ($r = .0056$, NS); or states' child population living below poverty level ($r = -.0888$, NS).

Need and Prevention Effort

Similar observations were made when association of these five indicators with prevention effort was tested. The only significant indicator was the proportion of children living below poverty level, which was negatively associated with prevention effort ($r = -.2761$, $p < .057$). No significant association was found with proportion of total child population in the states ($r = .2114$, NS); proportion of children living in out-of-home care ($r = -.0858$, NS); proportion of children involved in reports of abuse or neglect ($r = .1011$, NS); or with proportion of children living in single-parent families ($r = -.0417$; NS).

Resources and Expenditure Per Child

The states' resources, measured as per capita revenue, were found to be significantly associated with expenditure per child ($r = .3097$, $p < .037$). Upon further analysis, it was found that this association stemmed from per capita revenue from the federal government ($r = .4077$, $p < .008$). Association with per capita revenue from state taxes was not significant ($r = .0807$, NS).

Resources and Prevention Effort

Resources, however, were not significantly associated with prevention effort ($r = -.1687$, NS). Source of revenue was also not found to have any significant association with prevention effort (federal sources: $r = -.0690$; state taxes: $r = -.1465$).

Nonwhite Child Population and Expenditure Per Child

Proportion of nonwhite child population was found to be significantly but inversely associated with expenditure per child ($r = -.3402$, $p < .025$). It was also inversely associated with prevention effort ($r = -.2693$, $p < .062$).

In summary, the states' expenditure per child on child welfare services was found to be significantly associated with the proportion of federal and state contributions to states' child welfare expenditures. Expenditure per child was also found to be significantly associated with the status of the state child welfare agency in the state government structure, the states' per capita revenue from federal government, the proportion of child population, and the proportion of children living in single-parent families. It was negatively associated with the states' nonwhite child population (see Table 8).

Table 8
Variables Associated With Expenditure Per Child on Child Welfare Services

	Expenditure per Child		
	r	(n)	p
Proportion of federal contribution	.3983	(31)	.013
Proportion of state contribution	.3642	(30)	.024
Status of state agency	.3181	(29)	.046
Federal per capita revenue	.4077	(34)	.008
Proprotion of nonwhite children	-.3402	(34)	.025
Proportion of child population	.2524	(34)	.075
Proportion of children in single-parent families	.2417	(34)	.084

Prevention effort was associated with support from citizen groups and state government officials, and with the disposition of the state governor, key legislator, and child welfare director at .05 level of significance. At .1 level it was associated with support from members of state legislatures, and the proportion of federal contribution to states' child welfare expenditure. At this level it was also inversely associated with the proportion of children living below the state's poverty level and with the proportion of nonwhite children in the state (see Table 9).

Table 9 Variables Associated With States' Prevention Effort			
	Prevention Effort		
	r	(n)	p
Citizen groups' support for traditional services	.5413	(34)	.0001
State Government officials support for traditional services	.7217	(6)	.053
Legislative support for primary prevention services	.2740	(28)	.079
Disposition of the governor	.3602	(32)	.021
Disposition of the key legislator	.3071	(32)	.044
Disposition of the child welfare director	.3243	(30)	.043
Proportion of children living below poverty	-.2761	(34)	.057
Proportion of nonwhite children	-.2461	(34)	.080
Proportion of federal contribution	.2765	(31)	.065

Multivariate Analysis

Pearson's correlation coefficient indicates the separate association of each independent variable with the dependent variable. To study the collective effect of the independent variables associated with each dependent variable, multiple linear regression was conducted.

Expenditure Per Child

The independent variables associated with expenditure per child summarized above were tested for multicollinearity using Pearson's correlation coefficient. The only two variables found to be correlated were proportion of federal contribution and proportion of state contribution to states' child welfare expenditure ($r = -.7628$, $p < .0001$). Since the purpose was to study the role of federal funds on states' child welfare services, it was decided to use the proportion of federal contribution in the regression equation. The variables entered in the regression therefore were: per capita revenue from federal government, proportion of federal contribution to state's child welfare expenditure, status of the state agency, proportion of children in the state, proportion of children in single-parent families, and proportion of nonwhite children in the state.

Together, these variables had a strong significant correlation with expenditure per child (Multiple R = .736, F (6,21) = 4.13, p < .007), and they explain 54.1% variance in states' expenditure per child. When adjusted for chance associations, they explain 41.0 % variance in this dependent variable (R^2 = .5410, Adjusted R^2 =.4099). Of the six independent variables entered in this equation, two emerge as significant predictors. Proportion of states' per capita revenue from federal government was found to have the greatest relative impact on per child expenditure (beta .417, p < .024). Holding all other variables constant, an increase of $1.00 in per capita revenue from the federal government could increase the states' per child expenditure by $0.16. The next highest relative impact was that of proportion of children in single-parent families (beta .346, p < .046). Holding all other variables constant, a 1% increase in the proportion of children in single-parent families could increase states' expenditure per child on child welfare services by as much as $444.11. The next highest relative impact, not statistically significant as predictors, was that of status of the state agency and the proportion of nonwhite children in the state. Proportion of states' child population had the least impact on its per child expenditure on child welfare services. These results of this regression analysis are presented in Table 10.

Table 10
Regression Analysis of States' Expenditure Per Child on Child Welfare Services

Independent variable	Regression coefficient (B)	Standard error	Standardize coefficient (beta)
Federal per capita revenue	.160*	.066	.417*
Proportion of federal contribution	38.99	34.01	.185
Status	11.67	7.91	.226
Proportion of children in single-parent families	444.11**	209.24	.346**
Proportion of nonwhite children	-233.53	176.47	-.218
Proportion of child population	306.80	336.26	.15
Constant	87.67	103.15	

Multiple R = .7356
R^2 = .5410
Adjusted R^2 = .4099
* p < .024
** p < .046

N = 34.
Mean expenditure per child = $64.03
Standard error = 36.63

Prevention Effort

The independent variables associated with prevention effort at .05 level of significance were support from citizen groups, support from state government officials, the dispositions of the state governor, the key legislator and the child welfare director, and the proportion of children living below poverty level. Support from state government officials was not used in the regression equation as this existed in six states only, and missing data on this variable would have reduced the number of states in the equation considerably. The remaining five variables were tested for multicollinearity; none was found. The five variables thus entered in this regression equation were: citizen support, the dispositions of the governor, key legislator and the child welfare director, and the proportion of children living below poverty level.

Together, these five variables had a strong significant correlation with prevention effort (Multiple R = .7651, F (5,22) = 6.21, p < .001) and they explain 58.5% of the variance in states' prevention effort. When adjusted for chance relationships, they explain 49.1% of the variance (R^2 = .58536; Adjusted R^2 = .49113). Of these five variables, two emerge as significant predictors. Support from citizen groups had the greatest relative impact on prevention effort (beta .566, p < .0001). The next highest relative impact was that of the proportion of children living below poverty level (beta -.357, p < .029). This impact was negative; for a 1% increase in the proportion of children living below poverty level, prevention effort could decrease by as much as 75%, holding all other variables constant. Dispositions of the three implementors did not emerge as significant predictor variables (see Table 11).

Table 11
Regression Analysis of States' Prevention Effort

Independent variable	Regression coefficient (B)	Standard error	Standardize coefficient (beta)
Proportion of children below poverty level	-74.67	31.86	-.357*
Citizen suppport	14.26	3.71	.566**
Disposition of governor	4.08	3.13	.323
Disposition of child welfare director	1.90	2.35	.132
Disposition of key legislator	.684	2.69	.063
Constant	76.60	14.00	

Multiple R = .7651   N = 34.
R^2 = .5854   Mean Prevention effort = 39.7
Adjusted R^2 = .4911   Standard error = 17.08
* p < .029
** p < .0001

Summary

This chapter describes the statistical associations between variables. As all variables were measured at interval or ratio level, Pearson's correlation coefficient was used to measure associations. Multiple linear regression was conducted to test the collective impact of independent variables found to be correlated with expenditure per child and with states' prevention effort.

The propositions of variations between states in their child welfare expenditures and prevention effort are supported in the visual examination of tabular data. Being univariate data, statistical significance of this variation could not be tested. The proposition that states did not perceive P.L. 96-272 as an incentive for the development of primary prevention services was not supported; states in fact were divided in their perception of the significance of federal fiscal incentives and penalties in the increase in primary prevention services in states.

States' expenditure per child on child welfare services was significantly associated with proportion of federal contribution and with proportion of state contribution to states' child welfare expenditures. It was also significantly associated with the status of the state agency, states' per capita revenue from federal government, and proportion of nonwhite children in the state (negative correlation). Correlation of expenditure per child with two indicators of the state's need — proportion of child population and proportion of children in single-parent homes — was significant at .1 level, but no significant association was found with any other indicator of need. This expenditure also had no significant association with the political and ideological environment in the state or with the disposition of its state-level implementors. In regression analysis, six independent variables — states' per capita revenue from federal government, proportion of federal contribution, status of the state agency, proportion of child population, proportion of children living in single-parent families, and the proportion of nonwhite children in the state — explain 54.1% variance in states' child welfare expenditures. Two variables emerge as predictors; these were the states' per capita revenue from the federal government, and the proportion of children in single-parent families.

States' prevention effort was not associated with its expenditure per child or its economic capacity, but it was associated with some indicators of its political and ideological environment — disposition of its governor, key legislator and the child welfare director. It was negatively associated with the proportion of the states' poor and nonwhite child population.

Regression analysis was conducted to study the collective effect of citizen support, disposition of the three implementors, and proportion of children living below poverty level on states' prevention effort. Together, these variables explain 58.5% variance. Support from citizen groups and the proportion of states' child population living below poverty level emerged as significant predictor variables.

VI

Conclusions, Discussion, and Recommendations

Conclusions regarding states' response to the mandate of prevention depend upon how this mandate is interpreted. The driving force behind P.L. 96-272 was concern for children being placed in foster care because no other services were available to families in trouble, and their drifting in the foster care system indefinitely with little permanence in their lives. The primary objective of P.L. 96-272 was to prevent the problem of foster care drift and to ensure permanence for children, preferably with their own biological families. This was to be achieved by preventing the entry of children into the foster care system by providing alternative services to families, and by moving the children out of the foster care system quickly and expeditiously, either reuniting them with their families under safer conditions or finding alternate permanent families for them.

The states in this study have responded positively to the mandate of preventing the problem of children lingering in foster care indefinitely. In 1978-79, prior to the enactment of P.L. 96-272, thirty of the thirty-four states in this study provided reunification and permanency planning services in at least half the counties of their state. By 1985-86 all the states had started these services in at least half their counties, and in over 80% of the states where they existed earlier they had increased. In the twenty-seven states for which this data was available, the mean number of children in out-of-home care had decreased by 17.7% as compared to 1978.

States' response to the mandate of preventing the entry of children into the foster care system, however, has been mixed. Preplacement prevention services for families identified to be at risk of out-of-home placement of children existed in at least half the counties in thirty-one states prior to the enactment of P.L. 96-272. By 1985-86, two additional states had started them in at least half their counties, and in twenty-seven states where they existed earlier, they had increased. One state did not yet have these services in even half its' counties. Primary prevention services, on the other hand, services which would prevent the development of risk existed in at least half the counties of nineteen states in 1978-79. By 1985-86 they had increased in seventeen states, and nine additional states had started such services in at least half of their counties. Six states did not yet have such services in even half their counties[3].

Thus child welfare services increased in the states in this study since the enactment of P.L. 96-272, but they increased differentially. In 1985-86, all thirty-four states in this study provided reunification and permanency planning services in at least half their counties, thirty-three states provided preplacement prevention services in at least half their counties, but primary prevention services were provided in twenty-eight states only. Furthermore, these states reported an inordinately greater amount of resources — whether money or staff time — having been expended on preplacement prevention and reunification services than on primary prevention services.

Why this mixed response? Federal government used to give matching funds to states for maintenance of children in foster care when the child was placed in care upon judicial determination that staying at home was contrary to the welfare of the child. With this Act, federal government attached more conditions to these funds, making their availability contingent not only upon judicial determination that staying at home was contrary to the welfare of the child, but also upon judicial determination that reasonable effort had been made to prevent the child's placement in foster care (preplacement prevention), and to return the child to the biological family (reunification). An additional condition was that states try to find alternate permanent families for children who could not be safely reunited with their families. To assist states in finding alternate permanent families for hard-to-adopt children, federal government offered adoption subsidies, the amount of which was to be determined by the states on a case-by-case basis. Thus, states were faced with the choice of either paying for their foster care costs themselves, or have matching funds from federal government if they could show that they had provided reasonable preplacement prevention, reunification, and permanency planning services. In addition, they could get additional federal funds in the form of adoption subsidies. Both the "carrot" — the availability of additional federal funds — and the "stick" — the loss of federal funds — applied immediately. Besides, federal regulations did not define "reasonable effort," leaving its determination to the local judges. The states already had a child welfare system in place that provided child protection, foster care, and adoption services, and a legal system in place for judicial determination of the necessity of placement. Federal requirements thus did not necessitate establishment of new systems but could be met with modifications in states' existing systems.

For primary prevention services, however, the federal "carrot" and "stick" did not apply immediately. States would have received additional funds only after the federal appropriations for child welfare services under Title IVB (not including the foster care and adoption subsidy payments) exceeded $141 million, and the penalties would have applied after the federal government appropriated $266 million for two consecutive years. In 1979, even though $141 million were authorized, only $56 million were appropriated. Federal government has not yet come even close to the baseline appropriation of $141 million. That states perceived their highest priority as preventing the loss of federal funds they were already receiving is indicated by about 75% of the respondents perceiving the potential of loss of federal funds as very significant or somewhat significant in the increase in preplacement prevention and reunification services in their state. Their next order of priority was to prove the existence of permanency planning services which not only prevented the loss of federal foster care funds but also brought additional funds to the states in the form of adoption subsidies. About 70% of the respondents perceived the potential of loss of federal funds as very significant or somewhat significant, and about 67% of the respondents perceived the increase in federal funds as very significant or somewhat significant in the increase in permanency planning services in their state.

Primary prevention services also increased, though in fewer states, even though federal fiscal policy did not make that a high priority. Twenty-seven states responded to the questions on role of federal fiscal incentives and penalties in the increase in primary prevention services. Of these, the stick — the potential of loss of federal funds — was perceived as very significant or somewhat significant by about 60% of the respondents, and the carrot — both the actual and the potential of increase in federal funds — was perceived as very significant or somewhat significant by almost half the respondents.

These findings indicate that federal grants using the carrot-and-stick approach can have a powerful influence in bringing about change in social services to children and families in the states. When both the carrot and the stick are applied, change is much faster. But even the promise of the carrot and the threat of the stick can apparently be influential in bringing about some change.

In her study of the influence of federal grants, Derthick (1970) argues that the federal grant system encourages the phenomenon of goal displacement behavior, that is, state and local behavior that is directed towards increasing federal funds rather than towards federally prescribed programmatic ends. That goal displacement may have occurred in the implementation of the mandate to prevent the entry of children into the foster care system is suggested by the shift in states from services with no time limit and long-term services to crisis-oriented and short-term services to families. Crisis and short-term services could legally prove that reasonable effort has been made to prevent the placement of a child in foster care. These services help families who normally function well but are faced with a crisis or a life problem of short duration; with some help they can be restored to their normal functioning state. But they do little for families with disabled parents, single-parent families, poor families and multiproblem families whose life problems are likely to be of longer, sometimes of life-long duration. Thus even if social work wisdom dictates delivery of comprehensive long-term services which have been found to be more effective with the clients of child welfare agencies (Jones, Magura and Shyne 1981), in the absence of such services crisis or short-term services would have to be provided just to satisfy the requirement of judicial determination of reasonable effort. In addition, the component of adversarialism, hallmark of the legal system, is introduced into the helper (social worker)-helpee (family) relationship, which is antithetical to the stated purpose of helping families stay together. Furthermore, this study did not explore whether or not additional resources were given to the states' legal systems for their expanded task of determining reasonable effort. If not, then these legal organizations were subject to all the organizational problems delineated by Montjoy and O'Toole (1979). If they were given additional resources, then some of the states' resources were expended on expanding their legal systems, which could have been used to expand social services, which could have prevented the need for placement. Thus in the way the fiscal incentives and penalties were implemented in 1985-86, P.L. 96-272 certainly appears to have been very conducive to goal displacement behavior in the states.

States' tasks have expanded with the additional mandates of P.L. 96-272 as well as a 67.7% increase since 1980 in reports of suspected neglect and abuse of children, but their resources to provide necessary services have not increased. States' expenditure on child welfare services increased by 1.7% in absolute dollar amount, but when adjusted for inflation, it had decreased by 7.8%. A recent study indicates that high caseloads and low resources have forced the public child welfare agencies to develop formal and informal policies of screening child abuse reports into priority categories. Sexual abuse was given the highest priority because that is where political pressure existed. Children as young as ten or twelve years of age were given low priority because they were old enough to run or fight back. Neglect reports were given the lowest priority, even though neglect, "deprivation of necessities," is most frequently associated with fatalities (CWLA 1986). So one way of preventing the entry of children into the foster care system has been to leave them in vulnerable and potentially dangerous situations.

There were few substantive changes in the states' child welfare systems in the wake of P.L. 96-272. The designated state agency was a large bureaucratic organization in most states, usually part of a larger umbrella organization whose director was a political appointee. Over 60% of the states reported no change in their child welfare agencies except increase in both the size and the caseloads of the staff. Their budgets also increased, but presumably this was related to the increased staff. In the states that reported change, findings were ambiguous, with both increases and decreases in the characteristics studied at both state and local levels. From the written comments of the respondents, however, P.L. 96-272 appears to have been influential in changing attitudes; a larger number of staff of the child welfare systems were perceived as believing in the permanency planning philosophy. In about half the states this Act was perceived as having increased the ability of child welfare advocates to influence an increase in services.

Though the states were similar in their organizational context, their expansion of child welfare services, and in their emphasis on reunification and preplacement prevention services, there was wide variation between them in their expenditure per child on child welfare services and in their prevention effort. Expenditure per child had no significant association with the states' political and ideological environment or the disposition of their state-level implementors. The only characteristic of the state agency that was significantly associated was its status in the state government structure. Findings regarding association between states' need for child welfare services and their expenditure per child on child welfare services are ambiguous. Correlation between expenditure per child and states' child population was significant only if the acceptable criteria of significance is extended to .1 level. (p=.075), but the correlation between expenditure per child and its population in out-of-home care, or the population at direct risk of out-of-home care was not significant even at this extended level of significance. An indirect indicator of need — proportion of children in single-parent families—was significantly correlated with states' expenditure per child on child welfare services at .1 level of significance (p=.084). This variable emerged in regression analysis as one of the two predictors of expenditure, but it was not significantly correlated with states' prevention effort.

The variable significantly correlated with the states' expenditure per child on child welfare services was the states' economic resources — their per capita revenue from the federal government — which emerged in regression analysis as the other predictor variable. This finding is congruent with Collins' (1967) finding of rising public assistance expenditure with rising income level of the state and Ozawa's (1978) finding of rising AFDC payments with rising per capita revenue of the state. But states' per capita revenue from state taxes was not related to its expenditure on child welfare services. This does not support Ozawa's finding of positive correlation between AFDC payments and states' tax revenue and Hudson's (1983) finding of positive correlation between states' mental health expenditure and their tax effort.

These findings lead to the conclusion that states' expenditure on child welfare services depended upon the per capita revenue they received from the federal government, and this expenditure was not significantly related to most of the indicators of need in the states or to the states' prevention effort. This absence of significant correlation between expenditure per child and prevention effort, combined with the proportion of children in single-parent families as a predictor of expenditure but having no significant association with states' prevention effort, suggests that the expenditure was on reunification and permanency planning services, and that children in single-parent families were more likely to be placed in out-of-home care.

For prevention effort, states' economic resources or any characteristic of the state agency were not significant but the proportion of federal contribution to states' child welfare expenditure was significant at .1 level of significance. (p = .065). A scattergram indicates that in twelve states, as the federal contribution to states' child welfare expenditure increased from 35% to 80%, states' prevention effort increased from 15% to 40%. The small number of states in this linear relationship did not permit further statistical testing and a definite conclusion.

Prevention effort was not significantly associated with any direct indicators of need, but proportion of children living below poverty level had significant inverse relationship with prevention effort (p = .057). In regression analysis this emerged as one of two predictor variables. Thus in states where the proportion of children living below poverty level was high and therefore the need was likely to be higher, prevention effort was lower. At .1 level of significance, states' proportion of nonwhite child population also had significant inverse correlation with prevention effort (p = .08). This finding is consistent with Collins' and Ozawa's findings of inverse correlation between nonwhite population and public assistance expenditure and AFDC payments, but not with Hudson's findings of no association between nonwhite population and mental health expenditure in the states. No significant correlation existed between proportion of nonwhite child population and child population living below poverty level.

Derthick (1970) argued that to prevent goal displacement behavior, indoctrination of state and local administrators so that they shared the values and program objectives of the federal policy was of great importance. This indeed is substantiated in this study; disposition of the implementors, the extent to which the state governor, the key legislator and the child welfare director agreed with the social values inherent in P.L. 96-272 was found to be significantly associated with the state's prevention effort. State officials' support for traditional child welfare services and state legislators' support for primary prevention services were also significantly correlated with prevention effort. But the variable with the greatest relative weight, the second predictor, was the support from citizen and professional groups in the state. Holding all other variables constant, a one unit increase in citizen support could increase prevention effort by fourteen units.

In summary, these findings lead to the conclusion that the resources a state could spend on child welfare services depend upon the per capita revenue it receives from federal government. But the distribution of these resources between prevention, treatment and rehabilitation depends upon federal fiscal incentives and penalties, the extent to which the citizen and professional groups lobby for these services in the state, and the extent to which state-level implementors agree with the social values inherent in P.L. 96-272. Poor children, likely to need more preventive services, get less, and children in single-parent families are more likely to be placed in out-of-home care.

Implications

Bower (1987) cites an old Cornish test of insanity as follows: the person to be tested is placed in a small room facing a sink in which there is a spigot, a pail underneath and a ladle in the pail. The spigot is turned on and the testee is told to keep the water from overflowing from the pail. The person who continues to ladle, however energetically and successfully, without attending to the flow from the spigot, is judged insane.

In emphasizing preplacement prevention, reunification and permanency planning services over primary prevention services, the states are like the testee who is ladling energetically but has not attended to the spigot. In the reality of the states the flow from the spigot has become stronger as is evident from the dramatic rise in reports of suspected abuse and neglect of children, the increase in proportion of children in single-parent families, and the increase in proportion of children living below poverty level as indicated in national demographic surveys. So no matter how much they invest in preplacement prevention, states cannot prevent the entry of children into foster care unless they begin to provide primary prevention services. Like the testee, no matter how energetically they ladle, they cannot prevent the water from overflowing until they attend to the flow from the spigot.

The need for primary prevention services and the futility of preplacement prevention services and reunification services in some cases — intervention after a family has become dysfunctional — is being recognized by more people in more states. But the implementation of these services depends upon the federal funds received by the states. In its present implementation of federal fiscal incentives and penalties, federal government gave a ladle but not the tools to reduce the flow of water from the spigot, and the states themselves either did not consider it their role or did not have the strength to do so.

In the absence of adequate primary prevention and long-term services, children are being left in vulnerable and potentially dangerous situations or are still being placed in out-of-home care unnecessarily, and since they can no longer stay in foster care indefinitely, they are often being returned home prematurely. More than one state has experienced public scandal over the death of a child returned home prematurely by the child welfare system. Practitioners in the field indicate an increase in repeat placements of children, suggesting that instead of multiple foster homes after the first out-of-home placement, children may now be experiencing multiple placements between their biological families and different foster homes. This is not congruent with the goal of permanence for children.

From the perspective of a federal legislator, these findings imply that to prevent the entry of children into the foster care system without leaving them in dangerous situations or situations that are "contrary to their welfare," and to achieve the goal of permanence for children, Congress must provide both fiscal incentives and fiscal penalties to the states to induce substantive changes in services to families. In addition, Congress must be alert to the risk of goal displacement behavior in state and local administrators, particularly when the penalties are perceived to be higher than the incentives. Federal legislators would be wise to consider funding primary prevention services specifically, and federal administrators would be wise to heed William's recommendation of devising effective management strategies to minimize goal displacement behavior.

From the perspective of the state legislators also it is crucial to be alert to the possible organizational problems and risk of goal displacement behavior at the local level if either the policy mandate is not specific or it is not accompanied by sufficient additional resources. This implies providing resources for the tasks they assign to their state agency, a need to oversee effective management strategies for minimizing goal displacement behavior at all levels of hierarchy in the child welfare system, and a serious consideration of the use of all kinds of incentives, tangible and intangible. Particularly when necessary resources and monetary incentives cannot be provided, use of intangible rewards and incentives becomes even more important. This implies a two-way communication system between the direct service staff and the state-level administrators and legislators, which would provide to the legislators and administrators an accurate understanding of the nature of incentives — tangible and intangible — that would be effective in their state.

The power of federal fiscal incentives and penalties and the risk of goal displacement behavior is important information from the perspective of child welfare advocates as well. The best way of ensuring successful implementation is to lobby for both incentives and penalties. From this perspective an efficient strategy would be to actively support the election of sympathetic federal and state leaders who believe in government responsibility for services to families, for these elected officials allocate resources, appoint directors of child welfare agencies, support and lobby for services in the Congress and in state legislatures, and provide oversight. Another strategy is to organize demonstration of support by citizen groups. This study found a strong correlation between citizen support and states' prevention effort. It is an effective tool for obtaining treatment (reunification) and rehabilitation (permanency planning) services whose absence can create crises and public scandal, but it is less effective in getting primary prevention services as found in this study. Persuading "nonbelievers" to spend money on services whose immediate social benefit cannot be measured quantitatively remains difficult.

The two predictors for states' prevention effort were proportion of children living below poverty level and citizen support in the state legislature. From the perspective of social work practice poverty in children is not an easily manipulable variable, but support from citizen and professional groups, their lobby in the states' legislatures is. Only two respondents identified the National Association of Social Workers and only one respondent identified the Children's Defense Fund as having lobbied for services in their state. In all other states the groups identified as having provided support were consumers and providers of services. From the perspective of social work practice thus this has been a neglected area, an area in which our professional community organization skills could be utilized to develop political constituencies in support of services to parents. To organize such a constituency, though, public opinion has to be mobilized.

In the mobilization of public opinion the role of the media cannot be underestimated. Over a hundred years ago the media was instrumental in the formation of the first Society for the Protection of Children in New York. A hundred years later, in the 1980s, media has proven its immense power in shaping public opinion even more strongly. Media now is not limited to newspapers as it was a hundred years ago. Radio, television and popular magazines can also be used to shape public opinion, and the message does not have to be limited to public service announcements or scandal stories. Prime time television shows in the last five years have changed public attitudes about physical and sexual abuse. Yet social work practitioners and academics write in professional journals for the benefit of other professionals, not for public consumption. Public media is a powerful tool that we, as a profession, have overlooked. It is time we pay serious attention to the use of media as a practice skill.

But before we begin efforts at influencing public opinion, we as a profession need to reexamine our position on prevention and our role in the continuum of services from primary prevention to rehabilitation. While some primary prevention programs such as Family Life Education have been incorporated into the programs of Family Service Agencies, an overwhelming majority of social workers work in the area of treatment and rehabilitation, intervening after a problem has been identified. Since primary prevention programs are intended to prevent problems from occurring, they would prevent, or certainly reduce, the need for social work as presently practiced. If we did indeed promote primary prevention, our roles and functions would have to change. As Rapaport stated, primary prevention programs involve all the social institutions in which people normally participate. But social workers in host settings such as hospitals and schools, instead of acting as consultants as she envisaged, have usually been relegated to a secondary function and status. Even in the Headstart program where social work could have played a pivotal role, it was conceptualized as that of a facilitator for educators and health services personnel (Zigler and Valentine 1979). For us as a profession, the task would be to develop practice models to participate in the delivery of primary prevention services without losing our identity or our status in host settings such as hospitals, schools, churches, day care centers and recreational facilities. This is being considered in the profession; one model of neighborhood-based continuum of services has been proposed by Brown et al. (1982).

The question being raised for discussion again is, will social work serve a residual or an institutional function in the twenty-first century society?

Recommendations for Further Research

This is an exploratory study with a relatively small sample; findings of this study need to be tested in further research. Further, being a single cross-sectional design, this study does not measure change in states. It is possible that some states have changed considerably even though they still do not provide all the services in at least half the counties of their state. In addition, this study asked for only the existence of services, not their adequacy. These questions need to be addressed in further research.

Proportion of federal contribution to states' child welfare expenditure and their prevention effort was found to have a positive linear relationship when federal contribution was between 37% and 80%. Since only twelve states fell in this range, a definite conclusion cannot be drawn from this one study, but this relationship needs to be tested with greater accuracy as these findings would have crucial impact upon federal and state contributions to financing of services for children and families.

A majority of states reported a shift from long-term services to short-term services, but this study did not clarify if this shift was in services to families or in services to children already in foster care. The latter could be indicative of prevention of children lingering in foster care indefinitely, as it would imply that children are being returned to their families or being placed in other permanent homes expeditiously. This needs to be explored in further research for an accurate assessment of states' response. In addition, practitioners' opinion regarding increase in recidivism rate needs to be tested empirically.

Summary

For social work practice, the findings of this study imply that to influence the implementation of P.L. 96-272 to prevent the entry of children into foster care we need to elect federal and state officials who believe in government responsibility for services to families, who will provide resources specifically for primary prevention services in addition to preplacement prevention services in the states. Election of such officials involves mobilization of public opinion and development of political constituencies in support of services to parents. This is a relatively new area of practice in social work; while community organization skills can be utilized, the profession also needs to give serious consideration to the use of public media as a practice skill, and both practitioners and academics need to consider publishing in popular magazines for public consumption and not restricting their wisdom to other social workers and academics by publishing in professional journals only. However, as we mobilize public opinion in support of prevention services, we also need to develop practice models that will shift our function from primarily that of treatment and rehabilitation to a continuum of services from primary prevention to rehabilitation, without loss of status or identity.

Findings of this study also imply a crucial need to be alert to the risk of goal displacement behavior in state and local officials. Any grant-in-aid program involves the risk of goal displacement behavior, but the risk is much higher when the penalties outweigh incentives. This implies a need for effective management strategies at all levels of government — federal, state, and local — to minimize such behavior, and the need for a two-way communication system especially between the direct service workers and the state administrators and legislators to identify and utilize appropriate incentives. Since fiscal resources are always scarce, the need to identify and utilize appropriate non-monetary and intangible resources is particularly high.

While this study focused on one federal legislation, its findings are likely be applicable to influencing the implementation of any social policy. However, this study is exploratory in nature. Its findings need to be tested, and further research needs to be conducted to address questions left unanswered in this study as well as the additional questions raised by the findings of this study.

APPENDIX

APPENDIX A

Letter Introducing Research and Researcher

Dear _____

    Relatively little information is known about the kind of programs that states have developed to address the problems of foster care and adoptions in the wake of The Adoption Assistance and Child Welfare Act of 1980. As the Administrator of child welfare services in your state, you are uniquely positioned to provide this information.

    I have been delighted to serve as consultant to Ms. Krishna Samantrai, a doctoral student in social policy, as she has developed a survey to collect and disseminate to the states this information. Naturally, information will be kept absolutely confidential. Results of the survey will be sent to each participant.

    I write to ask you to participate in this important study, which will collect information from each state and the District of Columbia. To make this as nonintrusive as possible upon your time, a questionnaire has been developed that should take roughly one-half hour to complete. If time pressures do not allow you to complete it, I would deply appreciate your nomination of another staff person in your Department. (In this latter case, please return the nominee's name and address on the attached form in the enclosed self-addressed stamped envelope.)

    The questionnaire will be sent to you (or your nominee) in about two weeks. Thank you for your collaboration in the study.

Sincerely,

Bruce S. Jansson, Ph.D.
Associate Professor

APPENDIX B

Letter Accompanying Questionnaire

Dear _____

Pursuant to a letter from Dr. Jansson regarding the study of influence of P.L. 96-272 on state child welfare programs, please find enclosed a copy of the questionnaire and a return self-addressed stamped envelope for your convenience. Could you please fill it out and return it by (date).

All responses are confidential. Neither individuals nor states will be identified in any written or oral reports of the findings. Your state's name on the top right hand corner of the questionnaire is only to assist me to correlate the correct demographic and budget data on your state that I am obtaining from public documents, so that the information received from you can be interpreted more appropriately in terms of the state's population characteristics.

This study is expected to contribute to knowledge about factors significant in implementation of intergovernmental social policy, particularly policy affecting the lives of children and families. Every addition to knowledge influences future directions; your knowledge and expertise in this area could contribute to the direction child welfare policy takes in the future. If you would like a summary report of the findings, please fill out the address label on the last page of this questionnaire.

Thank you very much for your time, effort and candor. If you have any questions or concerns, please feel free to call me at (telephone).

Sincerely,

Krishna Samantrai

APPENDIX C

Reminder Letter

Dear _____

A questionnaire for the study of influence of P.L. 96-272 on state child welfare services was mailed to you on (date). Perhaps you have not had time to fill it out yet.

I am well aware of the many demands on your time. But your knowledge as a leader in child welfare in your state is invaluable, and every piece of knowledge adds to influence future directions.

In case the questionnaire has not reached you or is not handy at this time, I am enclosing another copy. Another return self-addressed stamped envelope is also enclosed for your convenience. Could you please fill it out and return it by (date).

Thank you very much for your time and effort.

Sincerely,

Krishna Samantrai

APPENDIX D

Final Letter

Dear _____

This is regarding the study on influence of P.L. 96-272 on states' child welfare services. I have been communicating with you by letter and by phone in the last four months.

We have not yet received a completed questionnaire from you. I am fully aware of the many demands on your time; if you are unable to participate for any reason, would you please advise me, so we can proceed accordingly.

Thank you very much.

Sincerely,

Krishna Samantrai

APPENDIX E

Note of Thanks

Dear _____

Thank you very much for returning the questionnaire on study of influence of P.L. 96-272 on state child welfare programs. I am well aware of the many demands on your time. Your participation in this study and sharing of your knowledge is very greatly appreciated.

Your address label for receipt of summary of findings has been noted. These will be sent to you as soon as they are ready.

Sincerely,

Krishna Samantrai

APPENDIX F

Questionnaire

This questionnaire is part of a study of influence of the Adoption Assistance and Child Welfare Act of 1980 (hereafter referred to as PL 96-272) on delivery of child welfare services in states. If you would like a summary of findings of this study, please fill out the address label on last page.

For purpose of this study, child welfare services are defined as follows:

Primary prevention services: Services that would be available to the general population, such as telephone hotline, family/parent drop-in center, community education/awareness programs.

Preplacement prevention services: Services that would be provided to children and families identified to be at risk, for example through a report of child abuse/neglect, but the child was not removed from home.

Reunification services: Services to children and families when the child was removed from home, but plan was to return child to family as quickly as possible.

Permanency planning services: Services geared toward finding alternate permanent families for children when the biological family is unable to resume their care.

Section 1. In this section, we are seeking information on the nature and extent of child welfare services in your state before and after PL 96-272.

	Primary prevention	Preplacement prevention	Reunification	Permanency planning
Recognizing existence of local variations,				
1. Did child welfare services as defined above exist in at least half the counties in your state in 1978-79? (Please indicate **yes** or **no** in each column)	_____	_____	_____	_____
2. Did child welfare services as defined above exist in at least half the counties in your state in 1985-86? (Please indicate **yes** or **no** in each column)	_____	_____	_____	_____

3. How would you characterize the *change* that might have occured in child welfare services in your state between 1980 and 1986? (Please **x** relevant category).

	Increased			No change	Decreased		
	A lot	some	A little	change	A little	some	A lot
Primary prevention services	❑	❑	❑	❑	❑	❑	❑
Preplacement prevention services	❑	❑	❑	❑	❑	❑	❑
Reunification services	❑	❑	❑	❑	❑	❑	❑
Permanency planning services	❑	❑	❑	❑	❑	❑	❑

If you indicated change in Preplacement prevention services, please answer question 4; otherwise please go to question 5.

4. In which kind of service did the change occur? (Please x relevant category/ies).

	Increased			No change	Decreased		
	A lot	some	A little	change	A little	some	A lot
Crisis intervention, services that could be delivered for upto one month.	☐	☐	☐	☐	☐	☐	☐
Short term, services that could be delivered upto six months.	☐	☐	☐	☐	☐	☐	☐
Long term , services that could be delivered for upto 18 months.	☐	☐	☐	☐	☐	☐	☐
Services that had *no time limit*, they could be delivered for as long as needed.	☐	☐	☐	☐	☐	☐	☐

If in question 3 you indicated change in any of the services (primary prevention, preplacement prevention, reunification or permanency planning), please answer question 5; otherwise please go to question 6.

5. How would you characterize the significance of following factors in causing or influencing this increase? Please **rank** them as follows:

   1 = very significant   2 = somewhat significant   3 = Little or no significance

	Primary prevention	Preplacement prevention	Reunification	Permanency planning
a. Increase in federal funds	_____	_____	_____	_____
b. Potential of increase in federal funds	_____	_____	_____	_____
c. Potential of loss of federal funds	_____	_____	_____	_____
d. Potential of restriction of federal foster care funds	_____	_____	_____	_____

Now we would like to have some information on your state child welfare expenditures and plan. Questions 7, 8 and 9 may be somewhat difficult to answer because, unlike any other questions, they involve estimates. Please make your best estimate in these questions if precise data is not available.

6. What was your state's child welfare budget for 1985-86?
   Total $ _____
   (Federal sources $_____ ; State funds $_____ ; Local sources $_____)

7. In your best estimate, what proportion of this total budget was spent on the following:

	Federal funds	State funds	Local funds	Total
Primary prevention services	_____	_____	_____	_____
Preplacement prevention services	_____	_____	_____	_____
Reunification services	_____	_____	_____	_____
Permanency planning services	_____	_____	_____	_____
All other expenditures	_____	_____	_____	_____
Total	_____	_____	_____	_____

8. In your best estimate, what proportion of staff time was spent on the following services, recognizing existence of local variations. (By staff we mean persons directly providing services to children and families).

	Primary prevention	Preplacement prevention	Reunification	Permanency planning	Total
Staff time	_____	_____	_____	_____	100%

9. In your best estimate, how much priority was given to the following services in IVB and IVE plans for **1986-87**? Please **rank** them as follows:

    1 = very high priority   2 = high priority   3 = somewhat   4 = hardly or none at all

	IVB	IVE
Development/Expansion of service information system	_____	_____
Compliance monitoring	_____	_____
Improvement in legal/court procedures	_____	_____
Improvement in service programs	_____	_____
primary prevention services	_____	_____
preplacement prevention services	_____	_____
reunification serviceS	_____	_____
permanency planning services	_____	_____
Other *(please specify)*	_____	_____

Section II. *In this section we would like to acquire some understanding of the child welfare system in your state, its structure, and how it functions.*

The following four questions solicit information on your state's child welfare law.

10. When was your state child welfare law (to comply with PL 96-272) enacted?

    month _____   year _____

11. Does your state law mandate minimum qualifications for line staff delivering services to children and families?

    ☐ Yes   ☐ No

    If yes, please **circle one** *of the categories below; otherwise go to next question,*

    1 = High School   2 = 2 years college
    3 = College degree, any major   4 = College degree, social work major
    5 = Master's degree, any major   6 = Master's degree in social work
    7 = Other *(please specify)*

12. Does your state law require, or make provisions for hiring of bilingual staff to deliver services? ☐ Yes ☐ No

13. Does your state law mention, make provisions for or mandate any of the following:
(please x relevant category/ies).

	Mentions	Provides for	Mandates
a. Primary prevention services	_____	_____	_____
b. Preplacement prevention services	_____	_____	_____
c. Reunification services	_____	_____	_____
d. Permanency planning services	_____	_____	_____

Now we would like to direct your attention to the child welfare system at state level.

14. In the structure of your state government in 1985-86, where was the designated IVB agency located? (please **circle** relevant category/ies)

a. A cabinet level department   c. Part of public welfare department

b. Part of a larger umbrella organization   d. A separate department

15. How was the Director of your state's IVB agency appointed? (please **circle one**)

a. At Governor's discretion   b. Civil Service Merit system   c. Other *(please specify)*

16. In your opinion, to what extent could the Director of the IVB agency influence state's budget allocations for child welfare services? (please **circle one**)

                 Great extent   Some   A little   Not at all

17. In your opinion, to what extent could the Director of the IVB agency influence the nature of child welfare services in the state, ie, degree of emphasis placed on primary prevention or preplacement prevention or reunification or permanency planning services? (please **circle one**)

                 Great extent   Some   A little   Not at all

If the state IVB agency was part of a larger organization (umbrella or public welfare department), please answer questions 18-22; otherwise please go to question 23.

18. How many programs was the larger organization responsible for? (please **circle one**)

               a = 2-4   b = 5-7   c = 8-10   d = over 10

19. What was the status of the state IVB agency in the larger organization? (please **circle one**)

a. Level 1: Division/Department in the larger organization
b. Level 2: Bureau in the Division/Dept. of the larger organization
c. Level 3: Office in the Bureau in the Division/Dept. of the larger organization
d. Other: *(please specify)*

20. How was the Director of the larger organization appointed? (please **circle one**)

a. At Governor's discretion
b. Civil Service Merit system
c. Other *(please specify)*

21. In your opinion, to what extent could the Director of the larger organization influence the state's budget allocations for child welfare services? (please **circle one**)

                 Great extent   Some   A little   Not at all

22. In your opinion, to what extent could the Director of the larger organization influence the nature of child welfare services in the state, ie, degree of emphasis placed on primary preventionor preplacement prevention or reunification or permanency planning services in the state ? (please **circle one**)

                                          Great extent   Some   A little   Not at all

Now we would like to direct your attention to the child welfare system at the local level, and the relationship between state agency and local public child welfare agencies.

23. Does your state require cities/counties to contribute funds to child welfare services at local level? (please **circle one**)

                      a = none   b = up to 10%   c = 11-25%   d = 26-33%   e = 34-50%   f = over 50%

24. In general practice at local level, what are the minimum qualifications of line staff delivering services to children and families ? (please **circle one**)

                              1 = High School   2 = 2 years college

                              3 = College degree, any major   4 = College degree, social work major

                              5 = Master's degree, any major   6 = Master's degree in social work

                              7 = Other *(please specify)*

25. How would you characterize local agencies' autonomy in defining "risk" situations to children and families, to which they will respond? (please **circle one**)

                            a = Great autonomy, state agency provides minimal requirements

                            b = Some autonomy, state agency provides general guidelines

                            c = Little autonomy, state agency provides strict guidelines

26. How would you characterize local agencies' autonomy in deciding what services will be provided, for example whether they will place more or less emphasis on primary prevention services or preplacement prevention services or reunification services or permanency planning services? (please **circle one**)

                            a = Great autonomy, state agency provides minimal requirements

                            b = Some autonomy, state agency provides general guidelines

                            c = Little autonomy, state agency provides strict guidelines

27. What mechanisms does the state agency use to monitor or supervise the local agencies'compliance with the state child welfare law ? (please x relevant categories)

	per month	per quarter	biannually	annually	other
Written reports					
Verbal reports					
Field visits by state officials					
Quality control/Assurance					
Other *(please specify)*					

28. What mechanisms does the state agency use when local agencies do not meet state requirements? (please **circle** relevant category/ies)

                            a = Written reprimand   e = Technical assistance

                            b = Verbal reprimand   f = Financial assistance

                            c = Threat of reduction of funds   g = Other *(please specify)*

                            d = Sanctions

29. Does the state have any mechanism to acknowledge, encourage, support or reward local agencies' success in preventing placement of children?　　　　　☐ Yes　　　☐ No
If yes, please describe briefly:

30. Since the enactment of P.L. 96-272, what changes have occured in the child welfaresystem in your state? (please **circle** relevant categories)

    a. *State agency:*

status in state government	elevated	lowered	no change
budget	increased	decreased	no change
size of staff	increased	decreased	no change
powers of the Director	increased	decreased	no change

    b. *Local agencies:*

autonomy in defining"risk"	increased	decreased	no change
autonomy in deciding kinds of service	increased	decreased	no change
size of professional staff	increased	decreased	no change
discretion/ autonomy of professional staff	increased	decreased	no change
caseloads	increased	decreased	no change

    c. *Ability of child welfare advocates in the state to influence:*

increase in programs	increased	decreased	no change
halt or reduce rate of cutbacks	increased	decreased	no change

---

> **Section III.** *In this section, we would like to get some understanding of political/ideological environment in your state.*

---

31. Considering the history of your state, would you say: (please **circle one**)

    > a = Your state is considered a leader in child welfare services
    > b = Your state has a history of extensive child welfare services
    > c = Your state has a history of average child welfare services
    > d = Your state has a history of minimal child welfare services

32. Considering the history of your state, how would you characterize its receptivity to federal direction? (please **circle one**)

very receptive	somewhat receptive	little receptivity	not receptive at all

33. In the period 1982- 85, did public media (major newspapers, TV) in your state carry stories on child protection, child abuse/neglect, foster care, and adoption related issues? (please **circle one**)

| great extent | somewhat | a little | not at all |

If there was any media coverage, please answer question 34; otherwise please go to question 35.

34. To what extent did media coverage influence changes in public child welfare service? (please x relevant categories)

	great extent	somewhat	a little	not at all
Primary prevention services				
Preplacement prevention services				
Reunification services				
Permanency planning services				

35. In your state in 1984-86, did any of the following individuals or groups support or lobby for services relating to child abuse/neglect, child protection, foster care and adoption? (please x relevant categories).

	very strong	strong	somewhat	none	against
State Governor					
Member(s) of state legislature					
State Govt. Official (s) *(please specify)*					
Local Govt. Official(s) *(please specify)*					
Citizen's groups/Professional					
Organizations *(please specify)*					
Other *(please specify)*					

36. In your state legislature in 1985-86, did any of the following individuals or groups support or lobby for primary prevention services? (please x relevant categories).

	very strong	strong	somewhat	none	against
State Governor					
Member(s) of state legislature					
State Govt. Official (s) *(please specify)*					
Local Govt. Official(s) *(please specify)*					
Citizen's groups/Professional					
Organizations *(please specify)*					
Other *(please specify)*					

37. Listed below are some statements. How do you think your State Governor in 1985, key state Legislator, Director of your state umbrella agency and Director of state IVB agency would respond to them? Please **rate** them as follows:

    1= strongly agree   2 = agree somewhat   3 = disagree   4 = strongly disagree

	Governor	Key legislator	Director Umbrella	Director IVB
a. Biological family is most important in care and upbringing of children; family ties should not be broken unless child's physical safety is at risk.	_____	_____	_____	_____
b. If parents cannot provide adequate care to their children, it is the responsibility of the government to help them do so.	_____	_____	_____	_____
c. Government should not wait till a family becomes dysfunctional to provide help. Comprehensive social services should be available to all families so that they do not become dysfunctional.	_____	_____	_____	_____
d. If a family cannot care for its children even with help, then it is the responsibility of the government to find alternate permanent families for the children.	_____	_____	_____	_____

*Thank you very much for taking the time to complete this questionnaire. **Any additional comments** about the child welfare services and expenditures in your state would be most welcome. If you would like a brief summary of the findings of this research, please fill out the address label below.*

Name: _____

Address: _____

Part II — From Secondary Sources

State name: _____   No. of counties: _____

In FY 1985-86
1. a. Total state expenditure: _____
    b. Total state population (July 1, 1985): _____

2. Total state revenue: _____
    a. Intergovernmental: _____ (Federal _____; Local _____)
    b. Taxes: _____

3. Revenue per capita: _____
    (Federal _____; Taxes _____)

4. a. State population:

	White	Black	Spanish-origin	Asian	Other	Total
	_____	_____	_____	_____	_____	_____

b. Child population:

	White	Black	Spanish-origin	Asian	Other	Total
under 5 years	_____	_____	_____	_____	_____	_____
5-9 years	_____	_____	_____	_____	_____	_____
10 to 14 years	_____	_____	_____	_____	_____	_____
Total (under 18)	_____	_____	_____	_____	_____	_____

5. No. children in single-parent families:

	White	Black	Spanish-origin	Asian	Other	Total
Female- headed	_____	_____	_____	_____	_____	_____
Male-headed	_____	_____	_____	_____	_____	_____
Total	_____	_____	_____	_____	_____	_____

6. No. children below poverty: _____

7. No. children involved in reports of child abuse/neglect:

1982	1983	1984	1985
_____	_____	_____	_____

8. No. children in out-of-home care:

1978	1985
_____	_____

NOTES

Introduction

1. The terms "foster care" and "out-of-home care" are used interchangeably.

Chapter I, Review of Literature

2. Sec. 471 (a) (15) . The Act only states "reasonable effort will be made..." but does not define it. Its definition has been left to judicial determination in states.

Chapter IV, Findings -- Description of the Data

3. This study asked for only the *existence* of these services, not their *adequacy*.

SELECT BIBLIOGRAPHY

Adam, Charles T. 1981. A descriptive definition of primary prevention. *Journal of Primary Prevention*. 2: 67-79.

The Adoption Assistance and Child Welfare Act of 1980. Public Law 96-272. *Statutes at Large of the United States of America*. 94 : 500.

Allen, MaryLee and Knitzer, Jane. 1983. "Child welfare: examining the policy framework." In *Child welfare: Current dilemmas, future directions*, edited by Brenda G. McGowan and William Meezan. Itasca, IL: F.E. Peacock Publishers, Inc.

Bardach, E. 1977. *The implementation game*. Cambridge, MA: Harvard University Press.

Barnard, Chester I. 1968. *The functions of the executive*. Cambridge, MA.: Harvard University Press.

Beck, Bertram M. 1959. *Prevention and treatment*. New York: National Association of Social Workers.

Bloom, Martin. 1980. A working definition of primary prevention related to social concerns. *Journal of Primary Prevention*. 1: 15-23.

_____. 1981. *Primary Prevention: The Possible Science*. Englewood Cliffs, New Jersey: Prentice Hall.

Bower, Eli M. 1987. Prevention: A word whose time has come. *American Journal of Orthopsychiatry*. 57: 4-5.

Bremner, Robert H., ed. 1971. *Children and youth in America: A documentary history*. Cambridge, MA: Harvard University Press.

Brown, June H.; Finch, Wilbur A. Jr.; Northen, Helen; Taylor, Samuel H.; and Weil, Marie. 1982. *Child, family, neighborhood: A masterplan for social service delivery.* New York: Child Welfare League of America.

Bullock, Charles S. III and Lamb, Charles M., eds. 1984. *Implementation of civil rights policy.* Monterey, CA.: Brooks/Cole Publishing Co.

Children's Defense Fund. 1978. *Children Without Homes.* Washington, D.C.

Collins, Lora S. 1967. "Public assistance expenditures in the United States." In *Studies in economics of income maintenance,* edited by Otto Eckstein. Washington D.C.: The Brookings Institutions.

CWLA. 1986. *Too young to run: The status of child abuse in America.* Washington, D.C.: Child Welfare League of America.

Dawson, Richard E. and Robinson, James A. 1963. Interparty competition, economic variables and welfare policies in the American States. *The Journal of Politics.* 2: 265-289.

Derthick, Martha. 1970. *The influence of federal grants,* Cambridge, MA.: Harvard University Press

_____. 1972. *New towns in-town.* Washington D.C.: The Urban Institute.

Etzioni, Amitai. 1965. "Organizational control structure." In *Handbook of organizations,* edited by James March. Chicago: Rand McNally.

Fanshel. D. and Shinn, E.B. 1978. *Children in foster care: A longitudinal study.* New York: Columbia University Press.

Federal Register. December 31 1980.

Federal Register. May 23 1983.

Geismar, Ludwig L. 1969. *Preventive intervention in social work.* Mituchen, N.J.: The Scarecrow Press.

Gilbert, Neil. 1982. Policy issues in primary prevention. *Social Work.* 27: 293-297.

Giovannoni, Jeanne M. 1982. Prevention of child abuse and neglect: Research and policy issues. *Social Work Research and Abstracts.* 18: 23-31.

Goldstein, Joseph; Freud, Anna; and Solnit, Albert J. 1973. *Beyond the best interest of the child.* New York; The Free Press.

Hage, Jerald and Aiken, Michael. 1970. *Social change in complex organizations.* New York: Random House.

Hargrove, Erwin C. 1975. *The missing link.* Washington D.C.: The Urban Institute.

Hastings, Margaret M. 1982. The politics of prevention. *Journal of Primary Prevention.* 3: 52-53.

Highlights. 1982, 1983, 1984, 1985. *Highlights of official child neglect and abuse reporting.* Denver, Colorado: The American Humane.

Hudson, Christopher G. 1987. An empirical model of state mental health spending behavior. *Social Work Research and Abstracts.* 23: 3-12.

Jansson, Bruce S. 1982. Ecology of preventive services. *Social Work Research and Abstracts.* 18: 14-22.

Jeter, Helen R. 1963. *Children problems and services in child welfare programs.* Washington D.C.: Children's Bureau and Child Welfare League of America.

Jones, Mary Ann; Magura, Stephen; and Shyne, Ann W. 1981. Effective practice with families in protective and preventive services: What works? *Child Welfare.* LX: 67-80.

Kahn, Alfred J. 1962. Therapy, Prevention and Developmental provision : A social work strategy. *Public Health Concepts in Social Work Education.* Proceedings of Seminar held at Princeton University, March 4-9, 1962. New York: Council on Social Work Education.

_____. 1979. *Social policy and social services.* Second edition. New York: Random House.

Klein, Donald C. and Goldston, Stephen E., eds. 1977. *Primary prevention: An idea whose time has come.* Rockville, Maryland: National Institute of Mental Health.

Kimmich, Madeleine H. 1983. *State child welfare program plans: Service budgets and expenditure reports.* Washington D.C.: The Urban Institute.

Koshel, Jeffrey J. and Kimmich, Madeleine H. 1983. *Summary report on the implementation of P.L. 96-272.* Washington D.C.: The Urban Institute.

Maas, Henry and Engler, Richard. 1959. *Children in need of parents.* New York: Columbia University Press.

McGowan, Brenda G. and Meezan, William. eds. 1983. *Child welfare: Current Dilemmas, future directions.* Prospect, Illinois: F.E.Peacock Publishers, Inc.

McCulloch, Patricia Clement. 1980. The ecological model: A framework for operationalizing prevention. *Journal of Primary Prevention.* 1: 35-43.

Meyer, Carol H. ed. 1974. *Preventive intervention in social work.* Washington D.C.: National Association of Social Workers.

Montjoy, Robert S. and O'Toole, Laurence J. 1979. Toward a theory of policy implementation: An organizational perspective. *Public Administration Review.* 39: 465-476.

Mott, Paul E. 1975. *Foster care and adoption: Some key policy issues.* Prepared for the Subcommittee on Children and Youth of the Committee on Labor and Public Welfare, United States Senate. Washington D.C.: U.S. Government Printing Office.

Nakamura, Robert and Smallwood, Frank. 1980. *The politics of policy implementation.* New York : St. Martin's Press.

National Commission on Children in Need of Parents. 1979. *Who Knows? Who Cares? Forgotten childen in foster care.* New York: Child Welfare League of America.

National Conference of State Legislatures. 1986. *Child welfare in the States : Fifty state survey report.* Denver, Colorado: National Conference of State Legislatures.

Ozawa, Martha N. 1978. An exploration into states' commitment to AFDC. *Journal of Social Service Research.* 1: 245-259.

Pike, Victor. 1977. *Permanent planning for children in foster care.* Washington, D.C.: U.S. Department of Health, Education and Welfare.

Pressman, Jeffrey and Wildavsky, Aaron. 1979. *Implementation.* Second edition. Berkeley, CA.: University of California Press.

Radin, Beryl A. 1977. *Implementation, change and the federal bureaucracy: School desegregation policy in HEW, 1964-1968.* New York: Teachers College Press.

Rapaport, Lydia. 1961. The concept of prevention in social work. *Social Work.* 6: 3-12.

_____. 1974. Working with families in crisis. In *Preventive intervention in social work,* edited by Carol H. Meyer. Washington D.C.: National Association of Social Workers.

Rein, Martin & Rabinowitz, Francine. 1977. *Implementation: A theoretical perspective.* Working Paper no. 43. Cambridge, MA.: Joint Center for Urban Studies of MIT and Harvard University.

Russell, Brenda L. 1984. "Child welfare policy." In *1983-84 supplement to the Encyclopedia of Social Work.* 17th edition. Silver Spring, Maryland: National Association of Social Workers.

Ryan, William and Morris, Laura. 1967. *Child welfare: Problems and potentials.* Boston, MA.: Committee on Children & Youth.

Sabatier, Paul and Mazmanian, Daniel. 1979. The conditions of effective implementation. *Policy Analysis.* 5: 481-504.

_____. 1980. The implementation of public policy: A framework for analysis. *Policy Studies Journal.* 8: 538-560.

Shyne, Ann W. and Schroeder, Anita G. 1978. *National study of social services to children and their families.* Washington D.C.: Children's Bureau, DHEW.

Sunley, Robert. 1968. "New dimensions in reaching out casework." In *Preventive intervention in social work,* edited by Carol H. Meyer. Washington D.C.: National Association of Social Workers.

U.S. Advisory Commission on Intergovernmental Relations. 1978. *Categorical grants: Their role and design.* Washington D.C.: U.S. Government Printing Office.

U.S. Department of Commerce. 1980a. *General Population Characteristics: 1980 Census of Population.* Washington D.C.: Bureau of Census.

_____. 1980b. *General Social and Economic Characteristics: 1980 Census of Population.* Washington D.C.: Bureau of Census.

_____. 1986. *State Government Finances in 1985.* Washington D.C.: Bureau of Census.

_____. 1986. *Statistical Abstracts of the United States.* Washington D.C.: Bureau of Census.

Van Horn, Carl E. and Van Meter, Donald S. 1976. The implementation of intergovernmental policy. In *Public policy making in the federal system,* edited by Charles O. Jones and Robert Thomas. Beverly Hills, CA.: Sage Publications.

Williams, Walter. 1980. *The implementation perspective.* Berkeley, CA.: University of California Press.

Wineman, David. 1959. "The life space interview." In *Preventive intervention in social work,* edited by Carol H. Meyer. Washington D.C.: National Association of Social Workers.

Zigler, Edward and Valentine, Jeanette. eds. 1979. *Project Headstart: A legacy of the war on poverty.* New York: The Free Press.

INDEX

Adam, 10

ADC, AFDC, 3-5, 23, 98-99
  See also Aid to Dependent
  Children

Adoption Assistance and Child
  Welfare Act of 1980, *x*, 5
  See also P.L. 96-272

Aid to Dependent Children,
  ix, 3-4, 22

American federalism, 11, 53
  incentives to states, 12-13
  grants to states, 12-14

Bardach, 19, 35

Barnard's theory of inducement,
  13

Beck, 9

Bloom, 10

Bower, 99

Bremner, 3

Bullock and Lamb, 24

Carrot-and-stick approach, *x*, 7,
  37, 73-75, 76, 78, 94-95

Child welfare services,
  definition of, 4
  in P.L. 96-272, 6
  in this study, 37

Collins, 23, 98

Cornish test of insanity, 99

Dawson and Robinson, 22

Dependent variables, *xi*,
  36-37, 39, 45, 79, 87-88

Derthick, 12, 14-15, 72, 95, 99

Etzioni's concept of compliance,
  13, 27

Fanshel and Shinn, *ix*

Federal funds for states' child
  welfare services, 4, 7, 29-30,
  46-48, 85, 89